AF412580

JIMMIE DURHAM

GOD'S CHILDREN, GOD'S POEMS

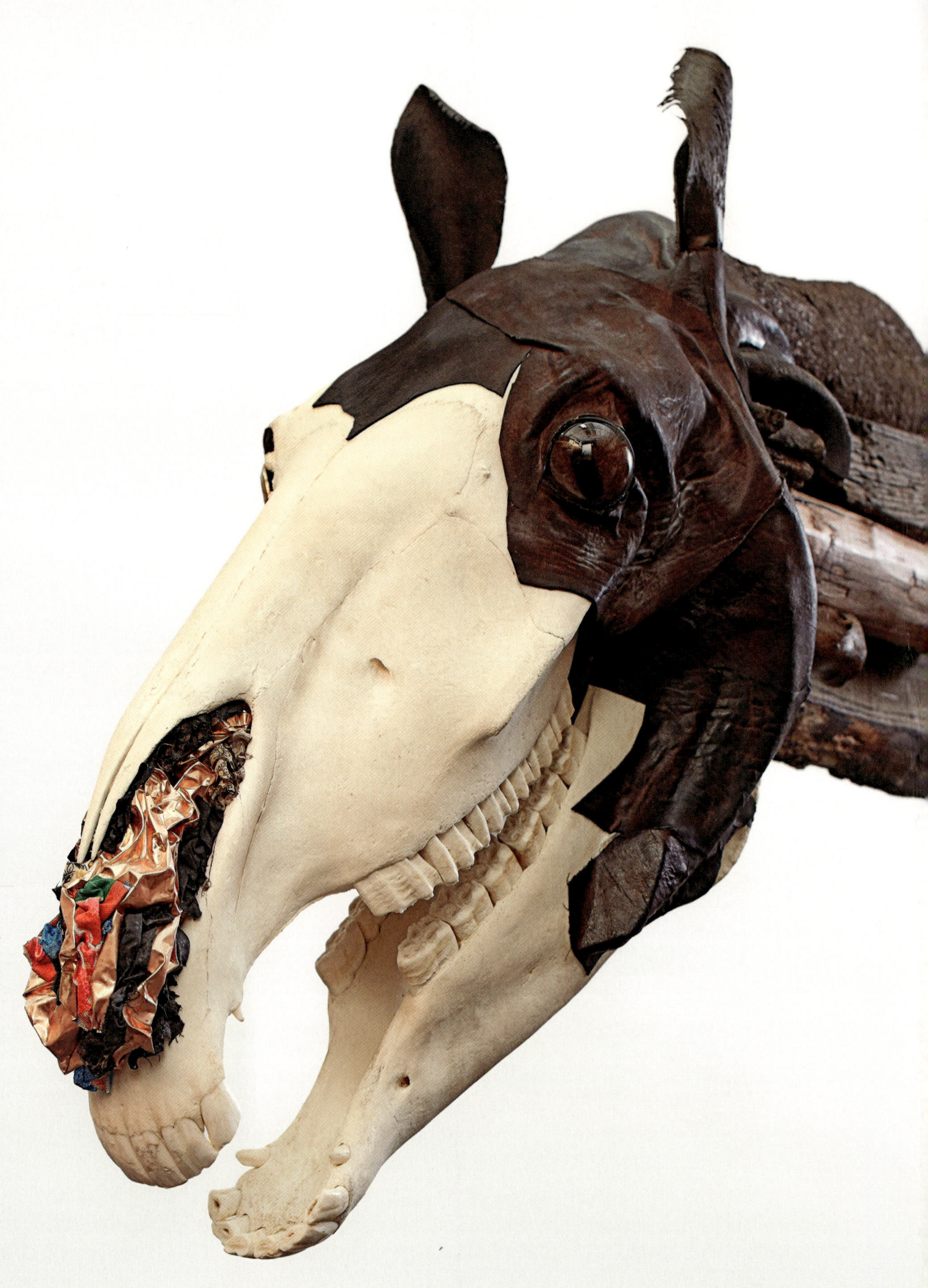

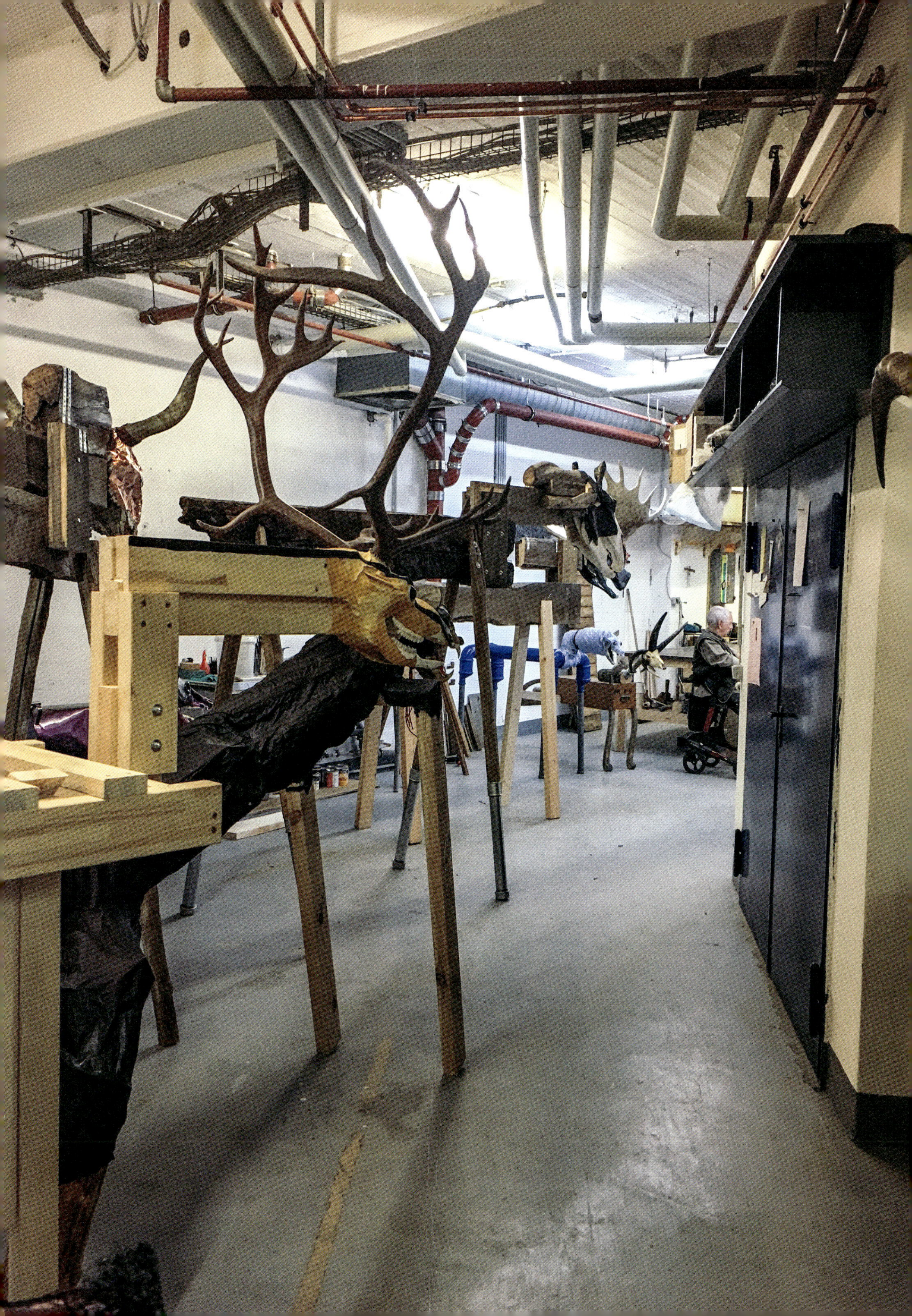

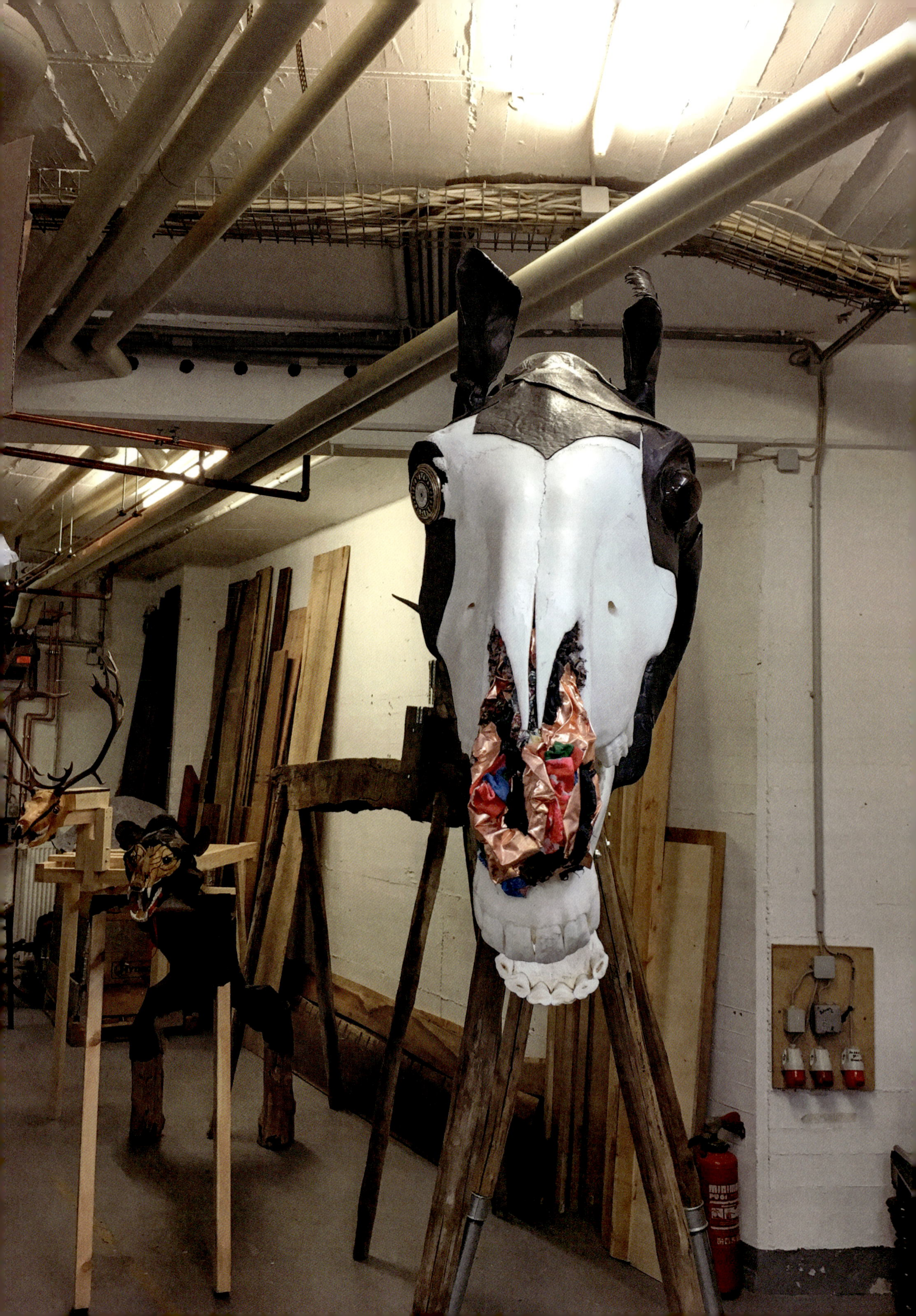

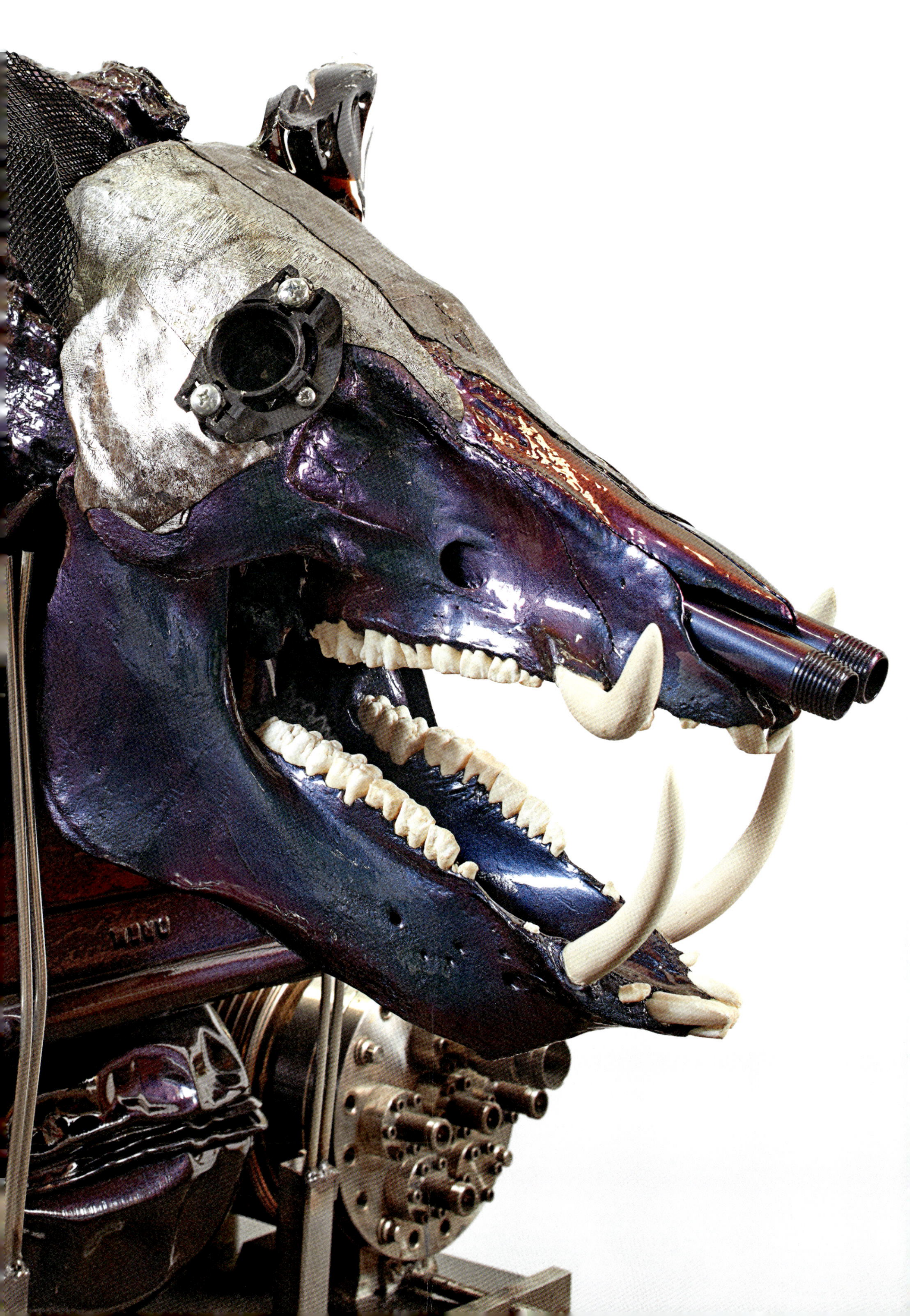

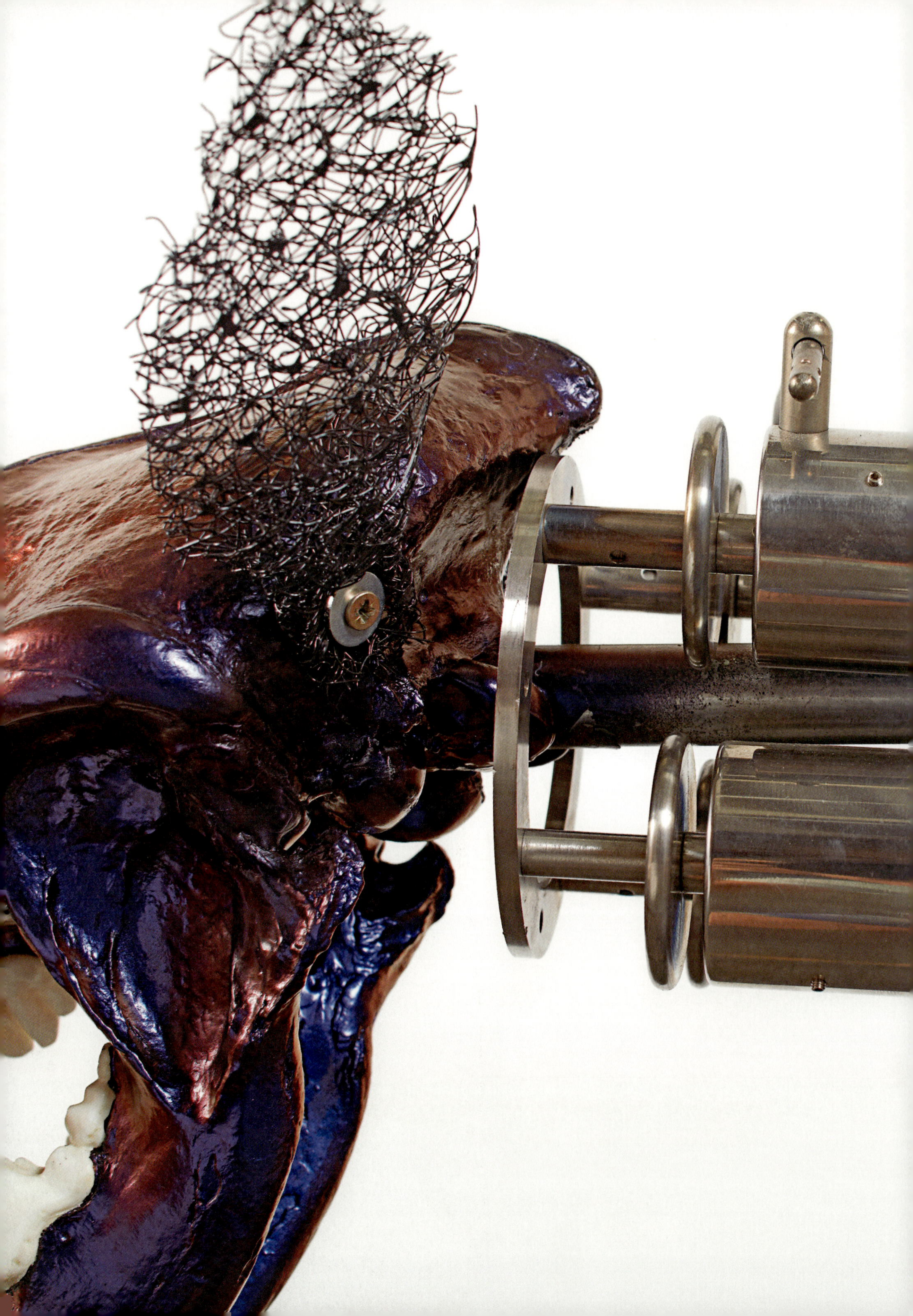

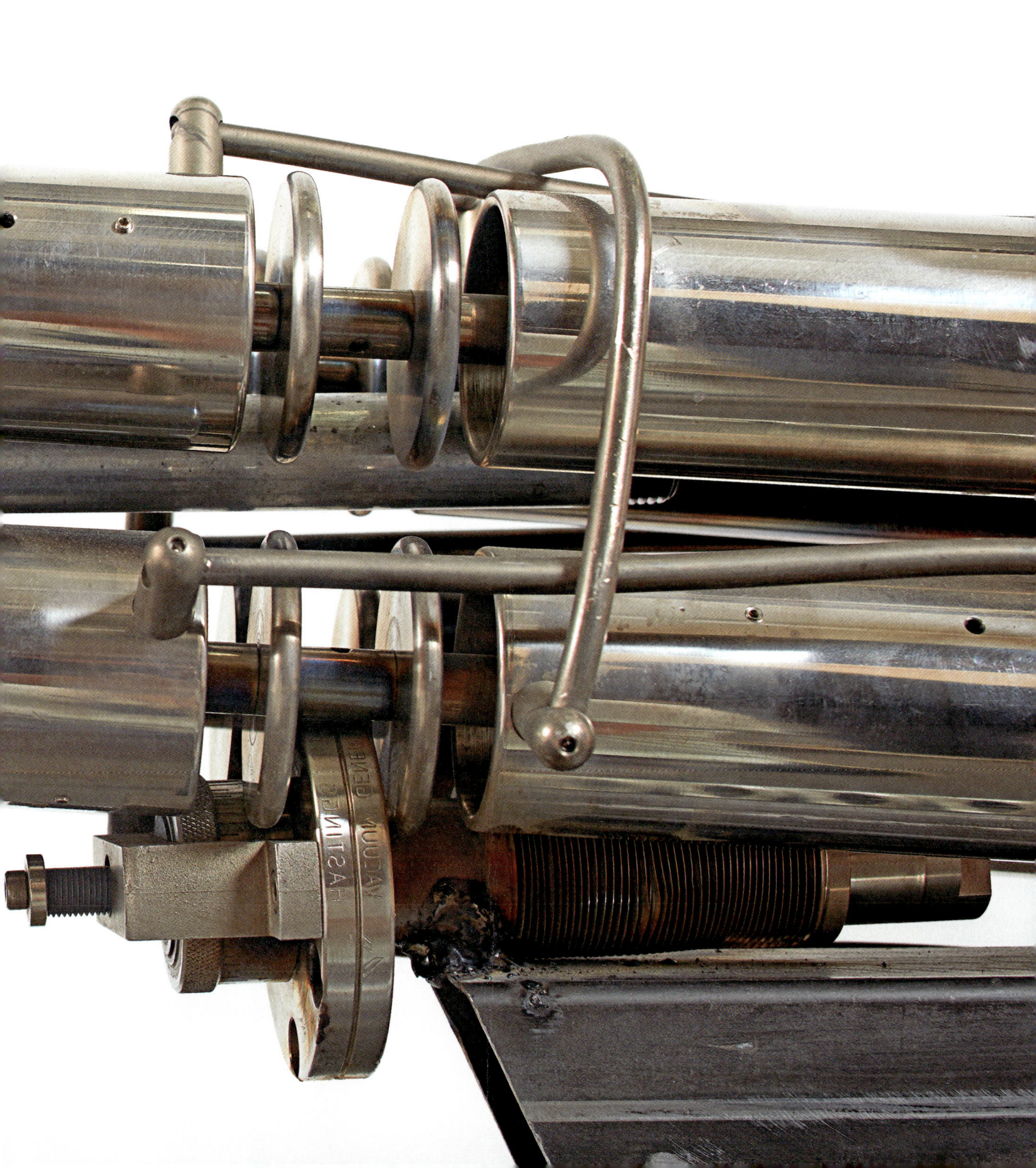

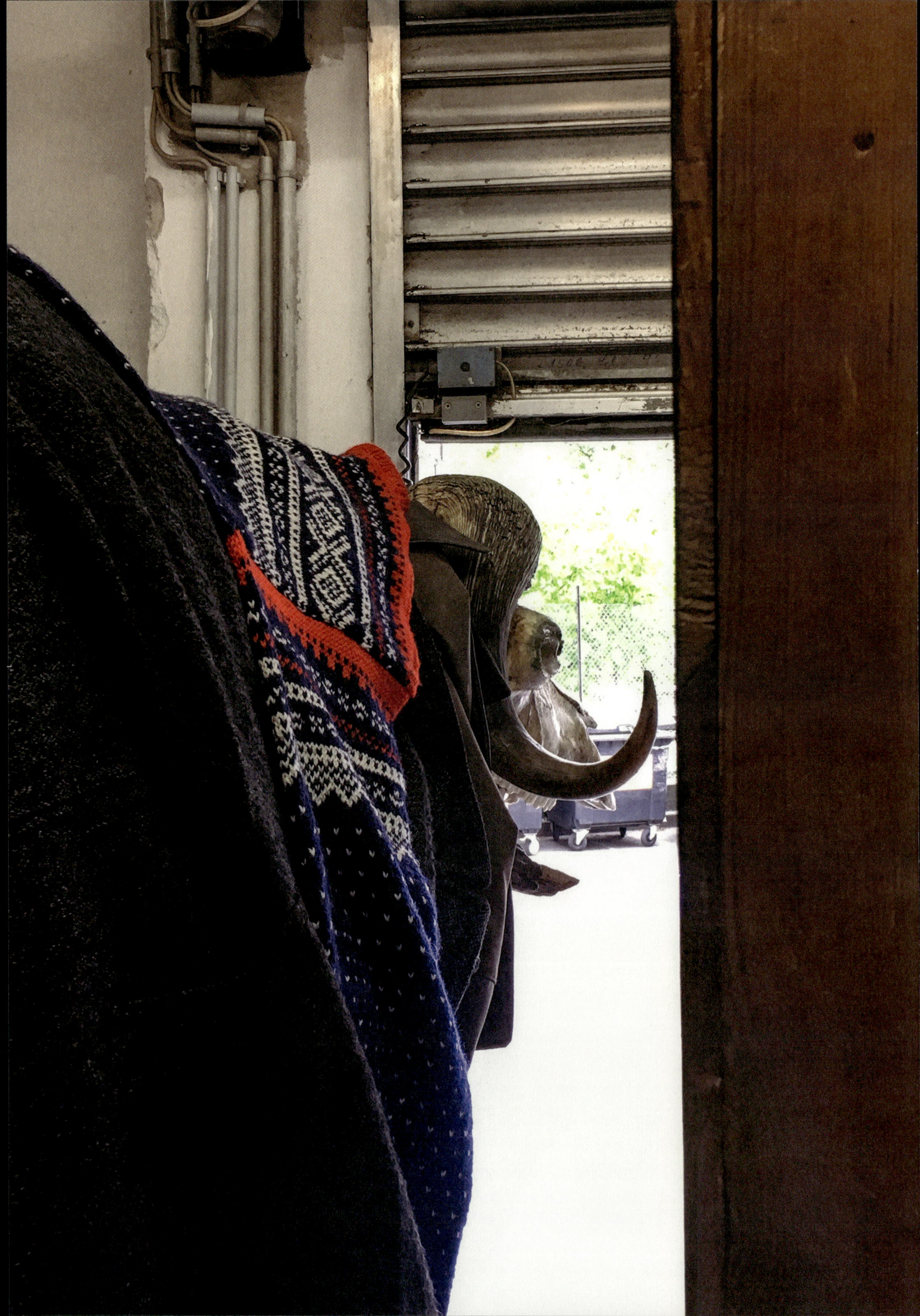

CONTENTS

Published by Migros Museum für Gegenwartskunst & JRP|Ringier

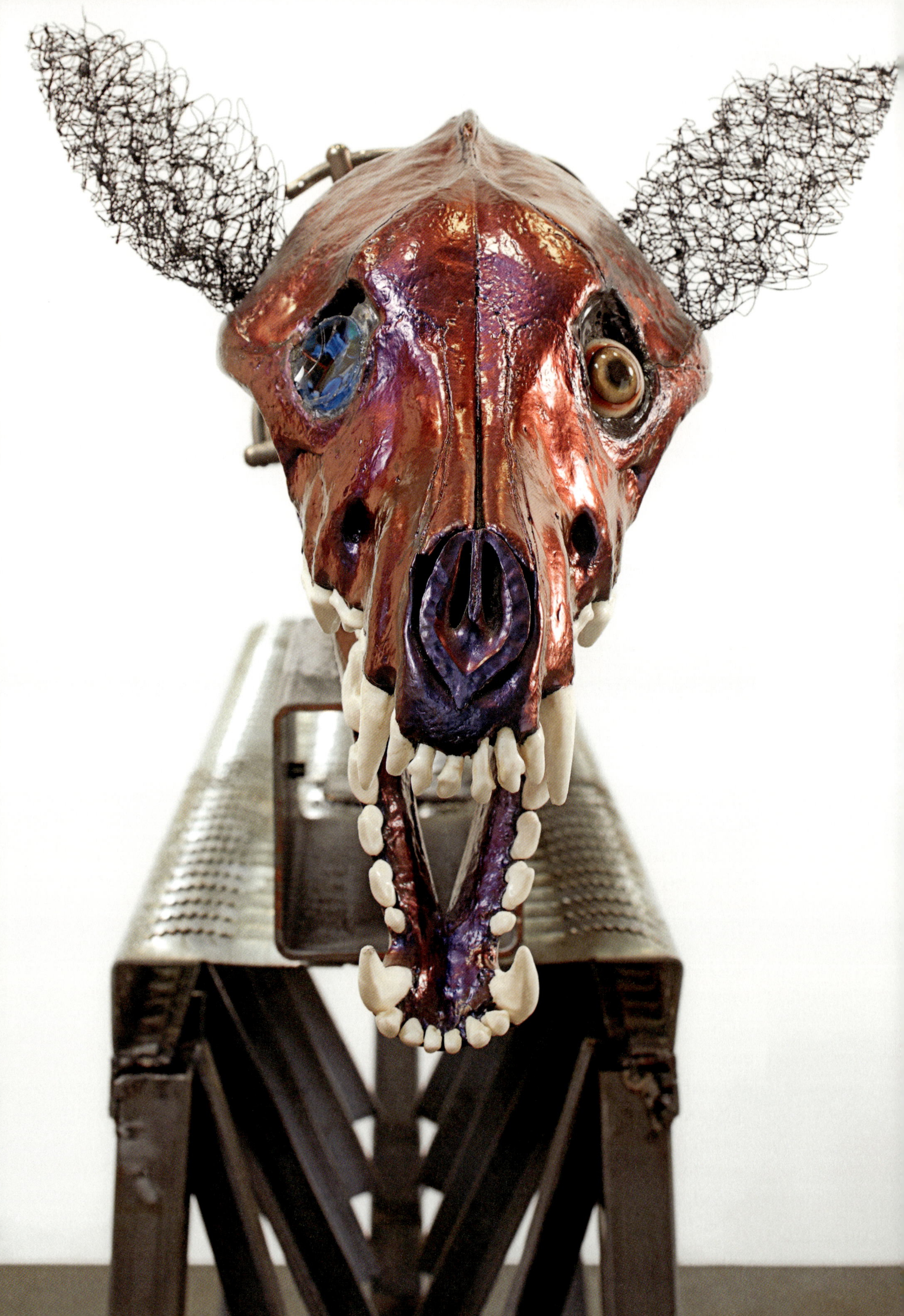

JIMMIE DURHAM

Soon after I first returned to Europe in 1994, Maria Thereza and I were by a horse pasture in the Netherlands. Among a group of normal horses there was a giant black stallion. I ducked under the fence, stupidly thinking to make friends with him. He ran magnificently from one end of the pasture to the other but would not stop and visit with a suspicious interloper.

I had seen the large workhorses of France and Ireland and of course the Clydesdales of the American brewery. But this horse was not a workhorse type—an extremely large running horse with the form and spirit of a good riding horse.

I have never forgotten that brief (and failed) encounter.

Some years later I saw cattle in Italy that were larger than seemed reasonable. There are two types of these huge animals; the Chianina, which is used now for beef, and the Maremmana. These two natural breeds are the remnants of the prehistoric aurochs of European cave paintings.

There is the skull of a Maremmana bull in this exhibit.

I wanted to gather the skulls of the largest animals of Europe and bring them back into our world by a method which I cannot explain, just as it is impossible to explain most music or poetry. The skulls I worked with all have bodies that are more sculptural than representative. I have the feeling that when using the actual bones, representation of the animal when it was alive would be too disrespectful to support.

The reasons for attempting such a thing as this are not really knowable. They would also be beside the point, not pertinent nor important.

Similarly, if I or anyone asks what I expect people to "get," to experience, from these pieces, an answer would have no relation to the question. They are made socially for us—for me and for anyone else who might see them, yet the complexity of each animal that I worked with remains with the piece. If I sing a song someone can ask, "Why sing that song here?" and the answer would have little to do with the question.

Scientists are just beginning to agree that we are now in the Anthropocene era. That is because an era is long, long, and we humans have hardly been around enough time that our heavy fists and feet would make the kinds of changes necessary to be called an era. One of the things scientists have been saying is, "If we all disappeared tomorrow would the Earth stay as we would have left it or would it quickly revert to some pre-human state?" It looks now, though, that it really would take millions of years to erase our prints.

Many people seem to think that by reporting on the Anthropocene in one way or another, they are somehow helping to alleviate its damage. (Or maybe they just like to say I told you so.)

Well, I wish always that science were more scientific. I have written before about how our knowledge comes from our bodies, our physical ways of experiencing the world. I wish science would stop taking humanity as the standard.

In what we call the "natural sciences"—biology, botany, chemistry, geology, etc.—the differentiation between humans and animals is still the law, even though most biologists will now say "other animals." This means that when we study intelligence, we use every ridiculous way to continually say that human, "our," intelligence is the standard. I must say that that does not seem very intelligent. Certainly our intelligence might be the proper standard for studying the intelligence of non-arboreal upright bipedal primates. But if we mean "rationality," or "logic," when we observe our behavior and how it has affected the world, we surely must see that our idea of our own intelligence must also be much more complex.

It does not matter if another type of animal is not like us in the areas of speech, reasoning, or such criteria, and everyone who has had a pet or friend animal of another species knows this. It is not anthropomorphistic. It is anthropocentric to imagine that we are the standard, that we are angelic, unearthly, or "higher" beings.

But we do constantly act anthropomorphically with our pets when we imagine them to be like us in the ways that are simian, if they are not simian. An adult dog is often called boy, or girl. Most animals become nervous at direct eye contact, but especially cats. When people who are not fond of cats look away from one, the cat takes it as a sign of friendliness and tries to reciprocate. This often makes the person describe the cat as cunning and manipulative.

But here is a truly strange and heavy phenomenon: any kind of land animal and many sea mammals will become a pet in the right circumstances. Doesn't it seem impossible and impossibly hard to bear that any animal will respond to human love and kindness? As though some god had given us, not dominion over other animals, but special responsibilities.

The title of this show of animal spirits is suggested by Koen van Synghel, a Belgian friend who read that the old Greek term for animals is "God's children" or "God's poems"; that is, the beloved works of God.

John Berger wrote a book titled, *Why Look at Animals?* When I first saw it, I thought it was a typically English way of thinking; Berger lived in rural France with farmers who depended on domesticated cattle and pigs for food and livelihood. Animals which were seen as food. His idea that people look at animals is not exactly typical of all humans, even in Europe. In Portugal people often regard animals just as friends, even if the person is a farmer.

When there are zoos, animal prisons, where people are specifically meant to look at animal prisoners, observation is the only possibility. And from that comes the television nature shows in which we watch animals without their knowing it. I think these ways of pretending to be with other animals are bad, but destructive as they are, they do show that we want to be connected to the world we live in.

I live in cities, and would not live anywhere else. For one thing, the number of stray dogs and cats in the countryside would be too heavy; my real reason, however, is the chance to be in the largest daily discourses without the censorship of family and friends: to be anonymous and human. But when we look at the world, it seems that humans have an instinct to make cities. Even a small community will construct barriers to keep intruders out and this is not bad: many of the would-be intruders are scorpions, poisonous snakes, biting and stinging insects, and mammals that will try to steal the groceries.

More and more, as we get comfortable in our cities, we begin to miss the rest of the world. Many people begin to work on this now, and plan ways that cities, and therefore ourselves, might be less separate.

Isn't it magic when you see a wild animal that is free in the forest or fields? And even more so when you see a wild animal in the city. Look! A fox! That happens often in Berlin and London, coyotes in Los Angeles. But otherwise we have endeavored to make our cities sterile and are not happy with the results.

People often like to call Europe a continent even though it is not by any geological definition. But because Eurasia is so vast, there are in fact animals specific to regions, and Europe has an abundance of animals large and small that are from here. It is the largest that I have tried to encounter with you.

EUROPA

JIMMIE DURHAM

Kurz nachdem ich 1994 das erste Mal nach Europa zurückgekehrt war, kamen Maria Thereza und ich in den Niederlanden an einer Pferdekoppel vorbei. Inmitten einer Gruppe normaler Pferde weidete dort auch ein prächtiger Rapphengst. Ich duckte mich unter dem Zaun hindurch und versuchte – naiv, wie ich war –, ihn anzulocken. Doch er rannte bloss immer wieder majestätisch von einem Ende der Weide zum anderen, machte aber keinerlei Anstalten, sich dem suspekten Eindringling zu nähern.

Bis dahin kannte ich nur die grossen Arbeitspferde in Frankreich und Irland und natürlich die Clydesdales der amerikanischen Brauereien. Aber dieses Pferd hier war kein Arbeitspferd, sondern ein extrem grosses Rennpferd, ein richtiges Reitpferd.

Ich habe diese ebenso kurze wie erfolglose Begegnung nie vergessen.

Ein paar Jahre später sah ich in Italien einmal eine Herde ungewöhnlich grosser Kühe. Dort gibt es zwei Rassen besonders stattlicher Rinder: die Chianina-Kuh, die heute vor allem als Fleischrind gezüchtet wird, und die Maremmaner Kuh. Diese beiden natürlichen Zuchtlinien stammen von den europäischen Auerochsen ab, die man aus prähistorischen Höhlenmalereien kennt.

Hier in der Ausstellung ist der Schädel eines Maremmaner Bullen zu sehen.

Ich wollte die Schädel der grössten europäischen Tiere sammeln und mithilfe eines Verfahrens, das ich so wenig zu erklären vermag wie die Wirkung eines musikalischen Werks oder eines Gedichts, wieder in unsere Welt bringen. Die Schädel, mit denen ich dabei gearbeitet habe, haben alle einen Körper, der allerdings nicht naturalistisch wiedergegeben ist, sondern sich skulptural präsentiert. Nach meinem Empfinden wäre es respektlos, das Skelett des betreffenden Tieres so wiederzugeben, wie es zu dessen Lebzeiten tatsächlich ausgesehen haben mag.

Die Gründe dafür anzugeben, warum ich so etwas mache, ist nicht so einfach.

Ausserdem wäre eine solche Erklärung deplatziert und weder sachdienlich noch wichtig. Das Gleiche gilt, wenn ich selbst oder ein anderer wissen will, was man denn von diesen Arbeiten «hat», was sie uns geben. Auch hier hätte eine mögliche Antwort mit der Frage nichts zu tun. Die Arbeiten sind für uns alle da – für mich und für jeden, der sie anschaut, dabei ist die Komplexität jedes Tieres, mit dem ich gearbeitet habe, Bestandteil der betreffenden Arbeit selbst. Wenn ich ein Lied singe, könnte jemand fragen: Wozu jetzt dieses Lied?, und die Antwort hätte mit der Frage so gut wie nichts zu tun.

Die Wissenschaften sind sich inzwischen darin einig, dass wir heute im Anthropozän leben. So ein Erdzeitalter dauert eigentlich sehr, sehr lange, dabei gibt es uns Menschen noch gar nicht lange genug, um die Veränderungen, die wir mit unseren schweren Fäusten und unseren Füssen anrichten, schon als Ära zu bezeichnen. Früher haben Wissenschaftler manchmal gefragt: Wenn wir morgen alle verschwunden wären, würden unsere Spuren dann noch längere Zeit auf der Erde sichtbar bleiben, oder würden die prähumanen Zustände schon bald wieder die Oberhand gewinnen? Inzwischen spricht allerdings fast alles dafür, dass unsere Hinterlassenschaften Millionen von Jahren überdauern werden.

Viele Leute scheinen zu glauben, dass sie die Schäden, die der Mensch auf der Welt angerichtet hat, wiedergutmachen können, wenn sie möglichst viel über das Anthropozän schreiben oder sprechen. (Vielleicht wollen sie damit aber auch nur ausdrücken: Siehst du, habe ich es dir nicht gesagt?)

Nun, ich wünsche mir oft, dass die Wissenschaft wissenschaftlicher wäre, als sie es ist. Ich habe bereits früher darüber geschrieben, wie es uns unser Körper, unser physischer Kontakt mit der Welt ermöglicht, Wissen zu erwerben. Ich wünschte, dass die Wissenschaft endlich aufhören würde, den Menschen zum Massstab aller Dinge zu machen.

In den sogenannten Naturwissenschaften – Fächern wie Biologie, Botanik, Chemie, Geologie – ist es immer noch

15

üblich, zwischen Mensch und Tier zu unterscheiden, obwohl die meisten Biologen heutzutage von «anderen Lebensformen» sprechen. Sobald wir uns mit dem Thema Intelligenz befassen, lassen wir uns bis heute von der lächerlichen Annahme leiten, dass die menschliche, also unsere eigene Intelligenz, der Massstab sei. Das wiederum erscheint mir nicht besonders intelligent. Möglich, dass unsere Intelligenz bei der Erforschung der Intelligenz der nicht mehr auf Bäumen lebenden, aufrecht gehenden zweibeinigen Primaten als Massstab dienen kann. Wenn wir jedoch Begriffe wie «Rationalität» oder «Logik» verwenden, um unser Verhalten und dessen Folgen für den Planeten zu beschreiben, müssen wir uns eingestehen, dass wir im Grunde genommen nur eine sehr beschränkte Vorstellung von unserer Intelligenz haben.

Es spielt nämlich überhaupt keine Rolle, ob andersartige Lebewesen uns etwa in puncto Sprachbegabung oder Reflexionsvermögen ebenbürtig sind, und jeder, der ein Haustier hat oder mit einem Tier befreundet ist, weiss das. Das ist kein Anthropomorphismus. Anthropozentrisch ist es vielmehr, zu glauben, dass wir der Massstab aller Dinge, dass wir engelsgleiche Wesen «höherer» Ordnung seien.

Dabei behandeln wir unsere Haustiere meist wie unseresgleichen, als ob sie uns wie die Affen, mit denen wir uns häufig vergleichen, ähnlich wären. So sagen wir beispielsweise zu einem erwachsenen Hund: «Good boy!», «Good girl!». Die meisten Tiere – vor allem aber Katzen – mögen keinen direkten Augenkontakt. Wenn ein Mensch, der Katzen nicht mag, in Gegenwart eines solchen Tiers den Blick abwendet, deutet die betreffende Katze das als Zeichen von Freundlichkeit und versucht, diese Freundlichkeit zu erwidern. Was häufig dazu führt, dass die betreffende Person die Katze erst recht für hinterlistig und berechnend hält.

Und noch etwas ebenso Merkwürdiges wie Bemerkenswertes: Beinahe alle Landtiere und viele Meeressäuger lassen sich unter den entsprechenden Bedingungen zähmen. Eigentlich unglaublich, dass fast alle Tiere auf menschliche Liebe und Zuwendung positiv reagieren. Als ob ein Gott uns zwar nicht zum Herrn, aber zum Hüter der Tiere bestellt hätte.

Der Ausstellungstitel *God's Children, God's Poems* stammt von Koen von Singhel, einem belgischen Freund, der irgendwo gelesen hatte, dass die alten Griechen die Tiere als «Gottes Kinder» oder «Gottes Poeme» (altgriechisch «poiema»: «Gemachtes», «Geschaffenes», «Komponiertes») bezeichneten, das heisst, als geliebte Geschöpfe Gottes.

Als ich zum ersten Mal den Titel von John Bergers Buch «Warum sehen wir Tiere an?» las, dachte ich: typisch englische Idee. Berger lebte in Frankreich auf dem Land unter Bauern, die Rinder und Schweine hielten, um ihren Lebensunterhalt zu bestreiten – Tiere, die als Lebensmittel gelten. Seine Idee, dass Menschen Tiere anschauen, ist nicht unbedingt typisch für alle Menschen, nicht einmal in Europa. In Portugal betrachten viele Leute die Tiere als Freunde, selbst die Bauern.

Im Zoo beispielsweise, also in einem Tiergefängnis, wo der Besucher die Tiersträflinge anschauen kann, ist Beobachtung die einzige Möglichkeit. Und daraus sind dann die Tiersendungen im Fernsehen entstanden, in denen wir Tiere beobachten können, die davon nichts ahnen. Ich halte nichts davon, sich auf diese Weise vorgeblich mit anderen Lebewesen abzugeben. Aber mag dieses Verhalten auch destruktiv sein, so zeigt es doch, dass wir mit der Welt, in der wir leben, in Verbindung stehen möchten.

Ich wohne in der Stadt und möchte auch nicht woanders leben. Zum einen weil mich auf dem Land die vielen streunenden Hunde und Katzen belasten würden. Der wahre Grund ist jedoch die Möglichkeit, in der Stadt ohne Bevormundung durch Verwandte und Freunde an einem mächtigen Diskurs teilzunehmen: anonym zu sein, einfach Mensch. Aber wenn wir die Welt anschauen, scheint es, als ob der Mensch einen Instinkt hat, der ihn drängt, Städte zu bauen. Selbst kleine Menschengruppen errichten Barrieren, um Eindringlinge fernzuhalten, und das ist auch nichts Schlimmes: Viele der Eindringlinge sind Skorpione,

Giftschlangen, stechende Insekten und Säugetiere, die uns unsere Lebensmittel wegnehmen wollen.

Sobald wir es uns dann in unseren Städten bequem gemacht haben, fehlt uns irgendwann die übrige Welt. Viele Leute befassen sich inzwischen mit diesem Thema und suchen nach Wegen, um die Abspaltung der Stadt und damit unserer selbst abzumildern.

Ist es nicht immer wieder ein magischer Anblick, wenn man in einem Wald oder auf einem Feld ein wildes Tier sieht, das völlig frei ist? Und – noch beeindruckender – wenn man ein wildes Tier in der Stadt sieht? Schau mal! Ein Fuchs! Das passiert in Berlin und in London ziemlich häufig, in Los Angeles sind es Koyoten. Doch ansonsten haben wir alles getan, um unsere Städte zu sterilisieren, und sind mit dem Ergebnis nicht recht glücklich.

Europa gilt allgemein als Kontinent, obwohl es das im geografischen Sinne gar nicht ist. Aber da Eurasien nun mal so riesig ist, kommen manche Tiere dort nur in bestimmten Regionen vor, und Europa ist die Heimat zahlloser grosser und kleiner Tiere. Das ist das Grösste, was ich mit euch erkunden wollte ...

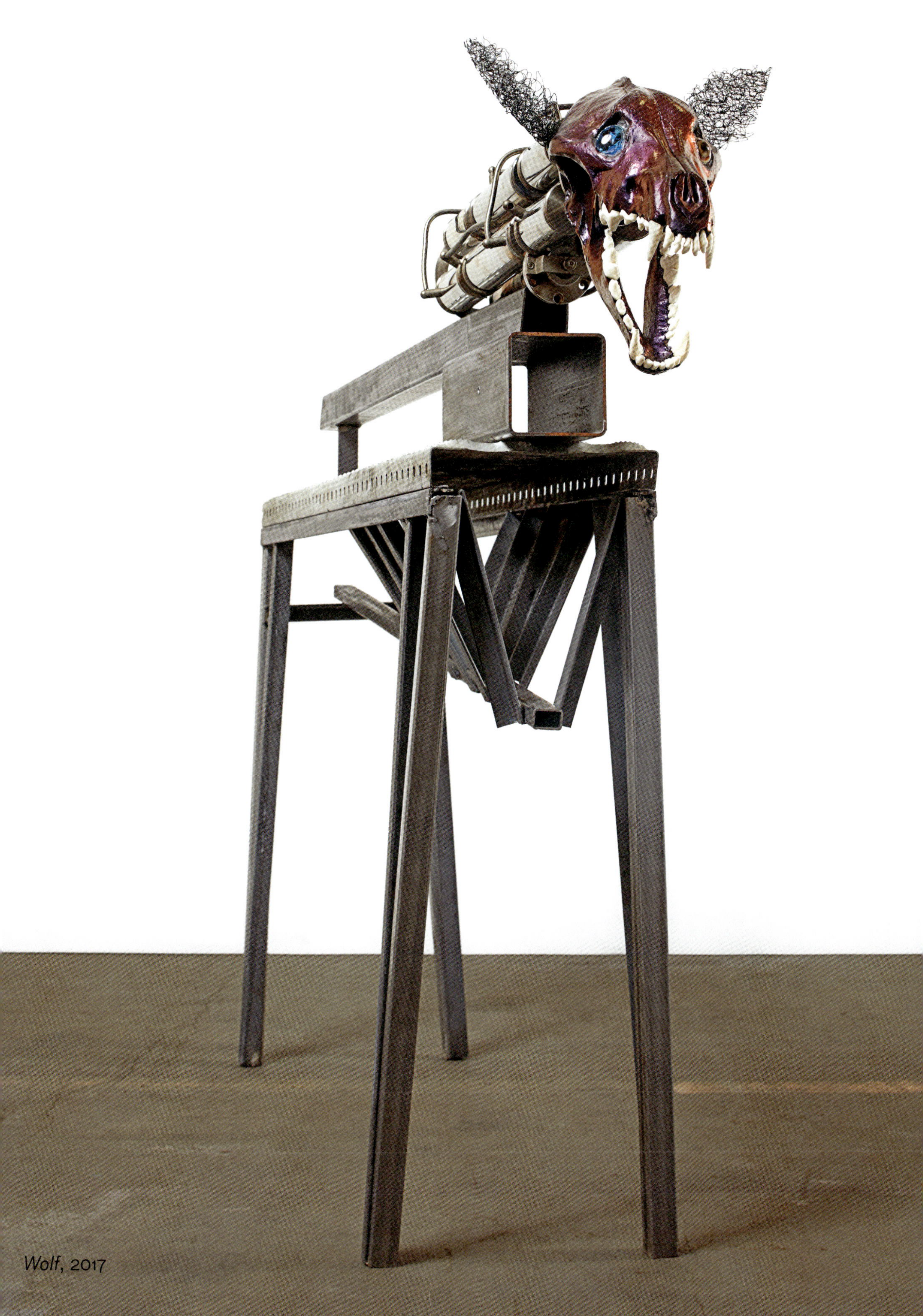

Wolf, 2017

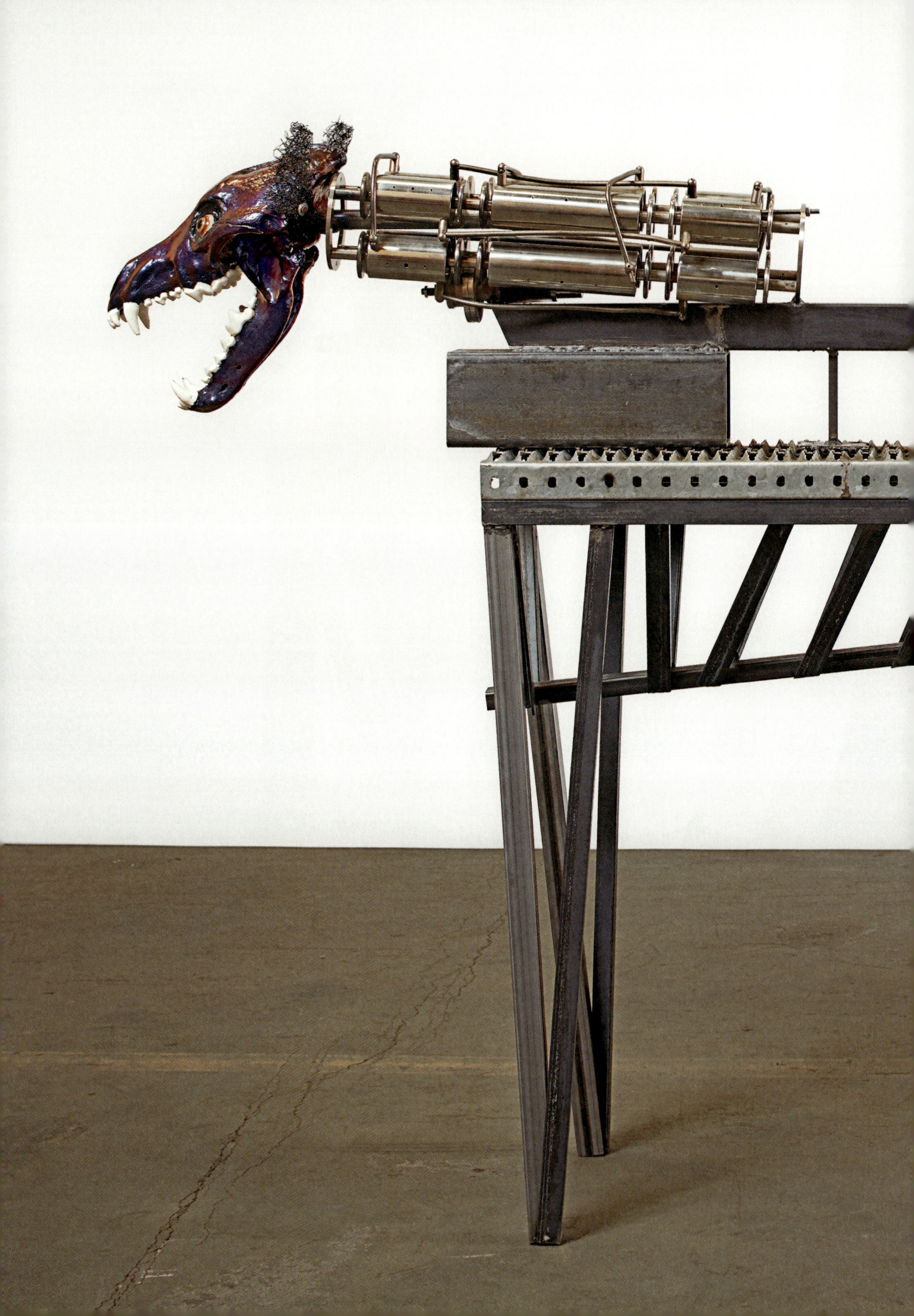

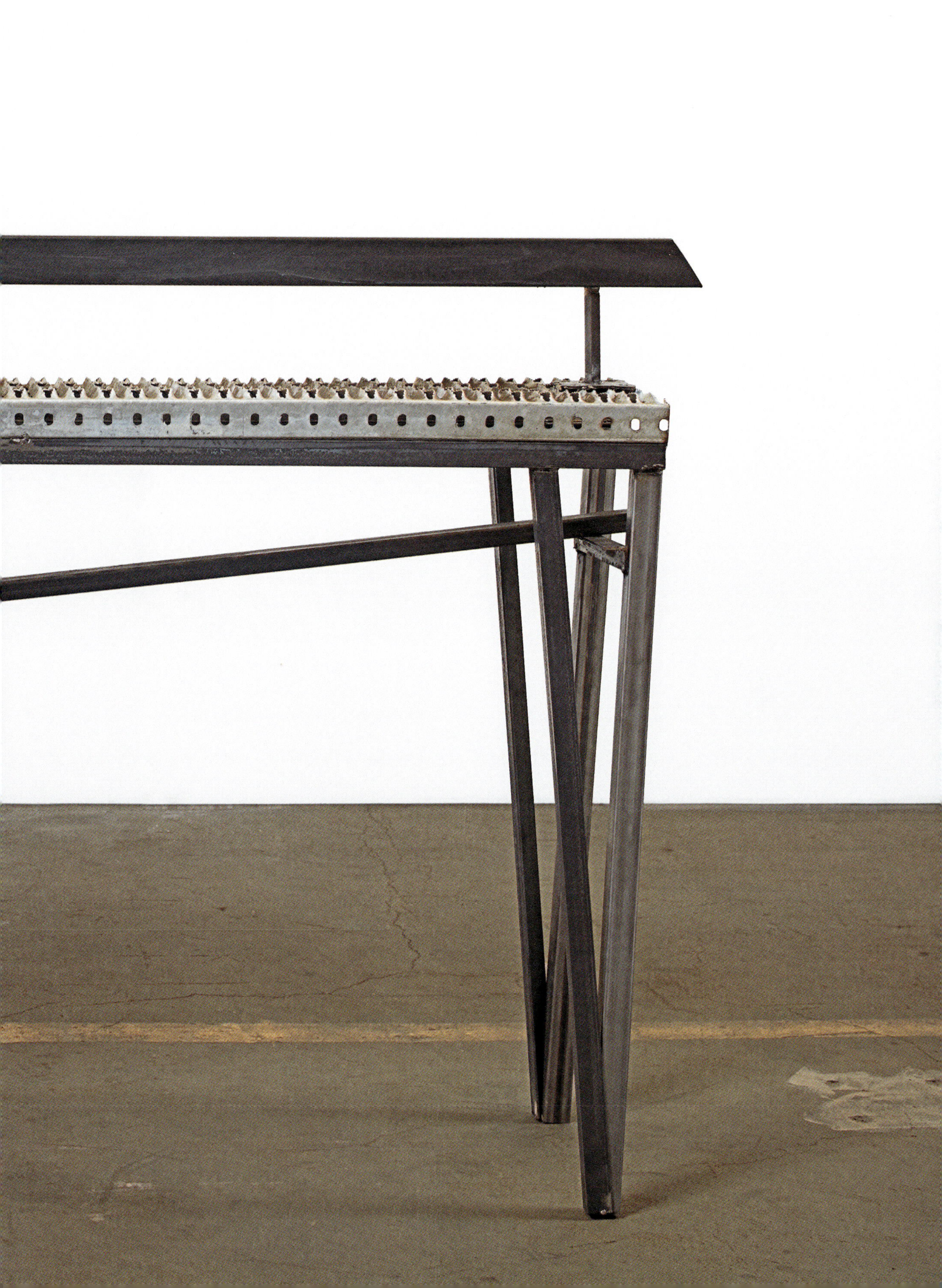

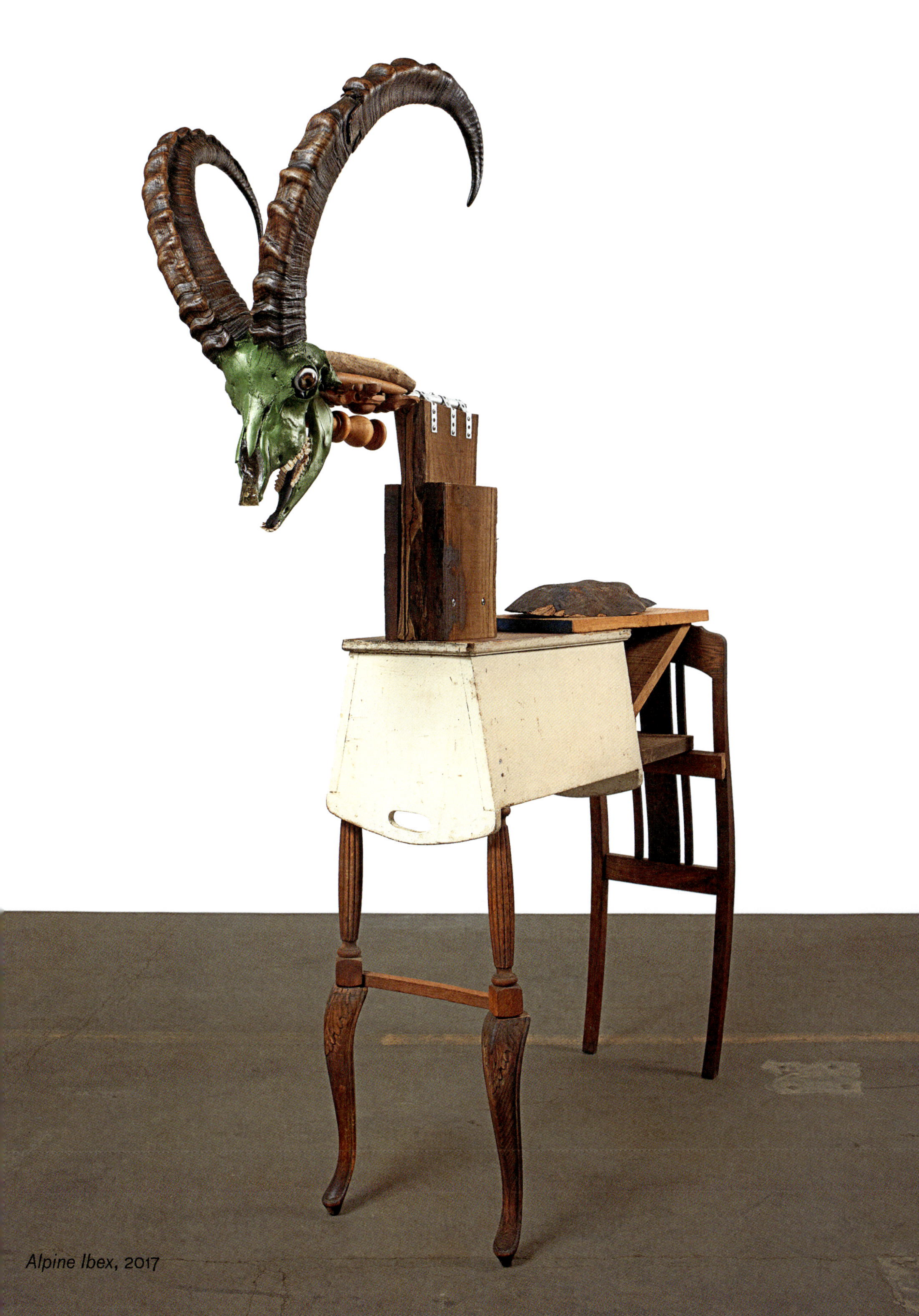

Alpine Ibex, 2017

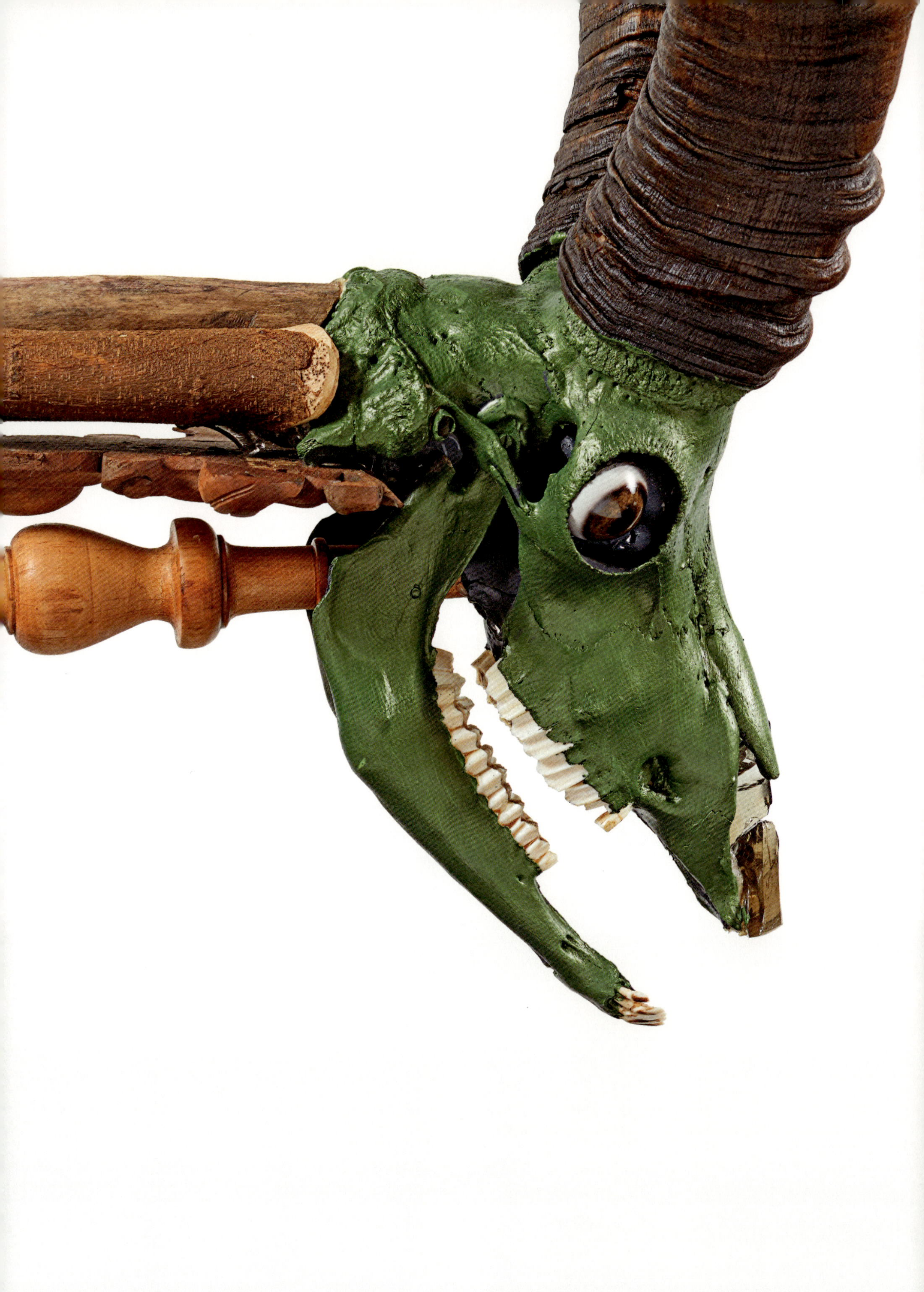

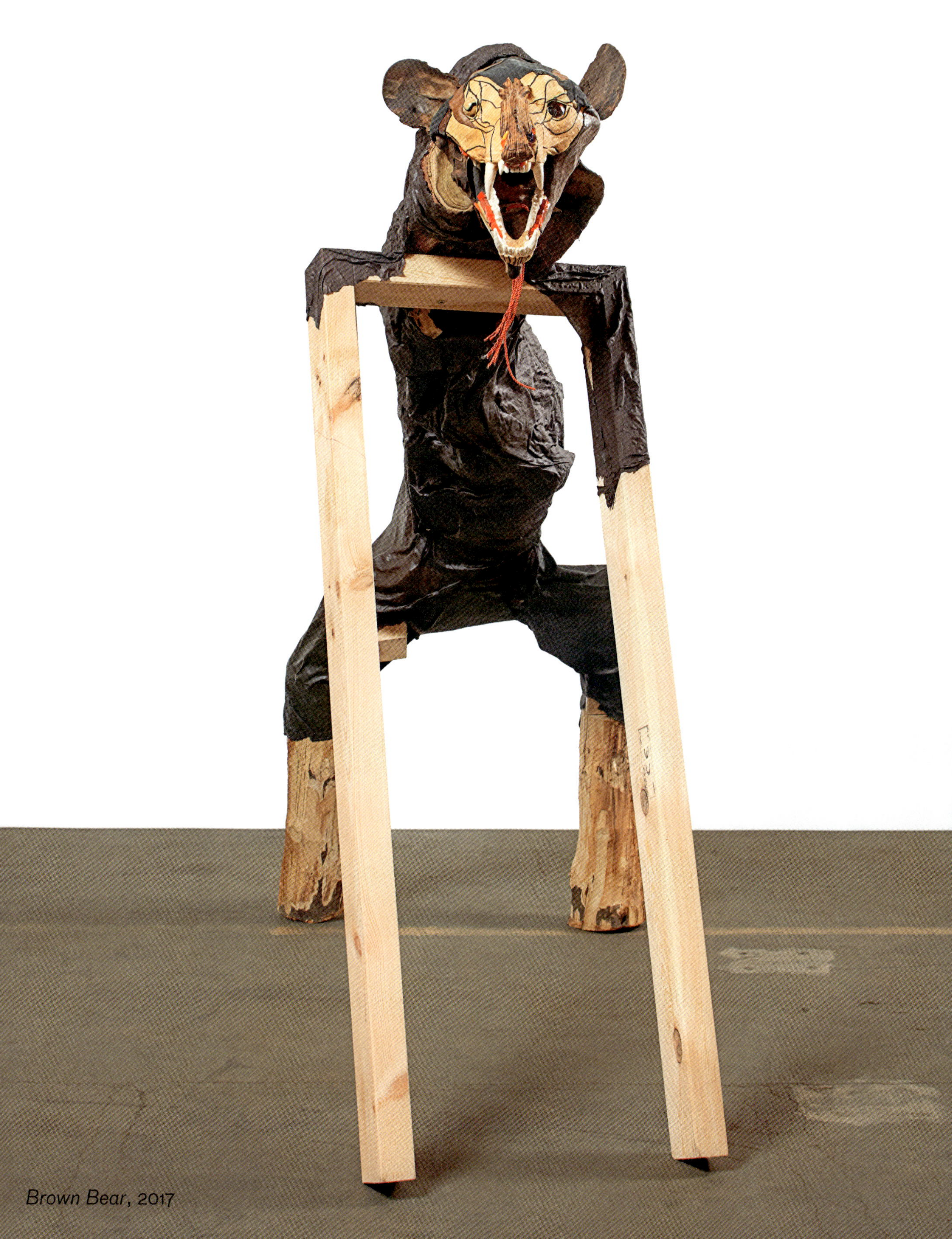

Brown Bear, 2017

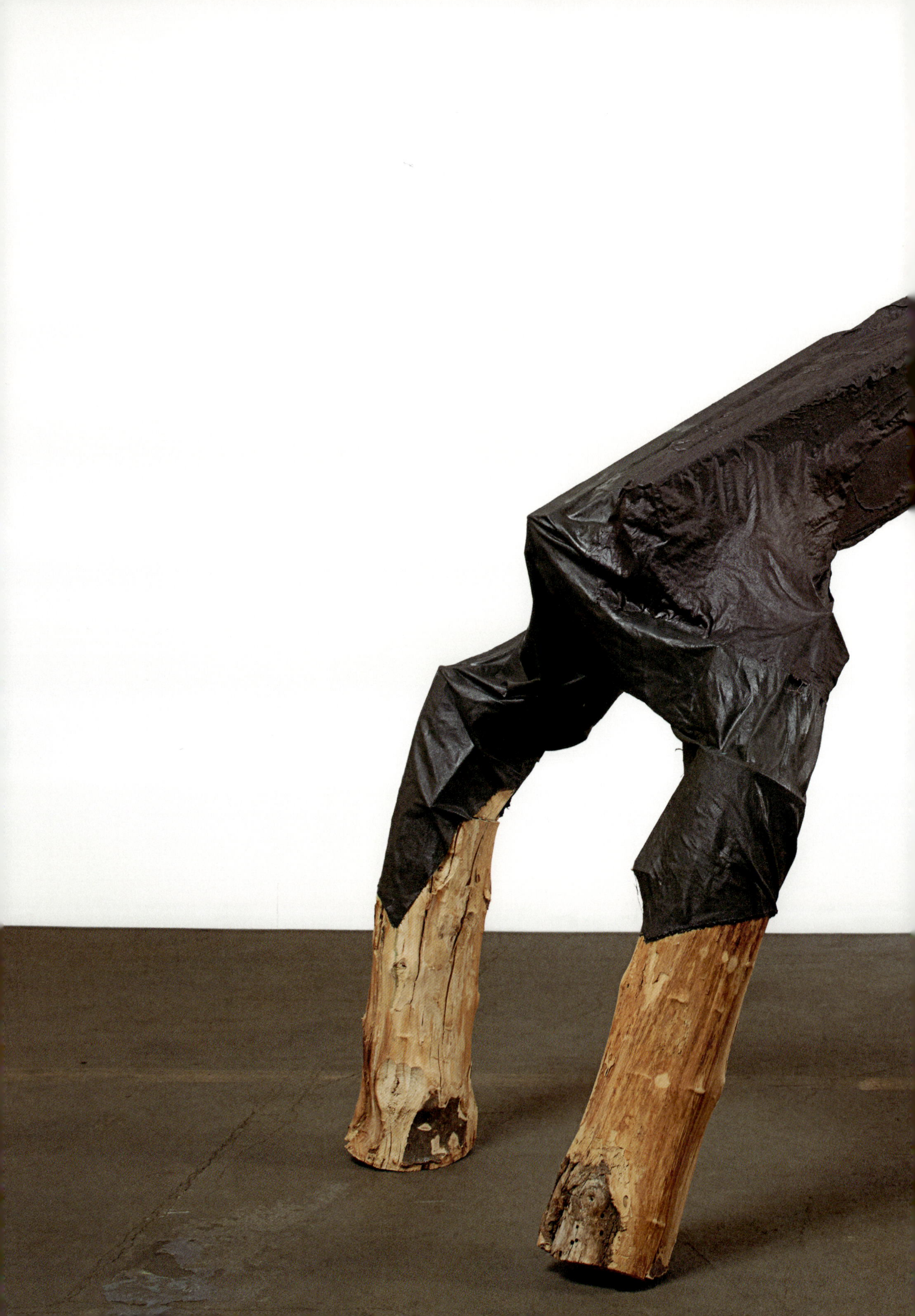

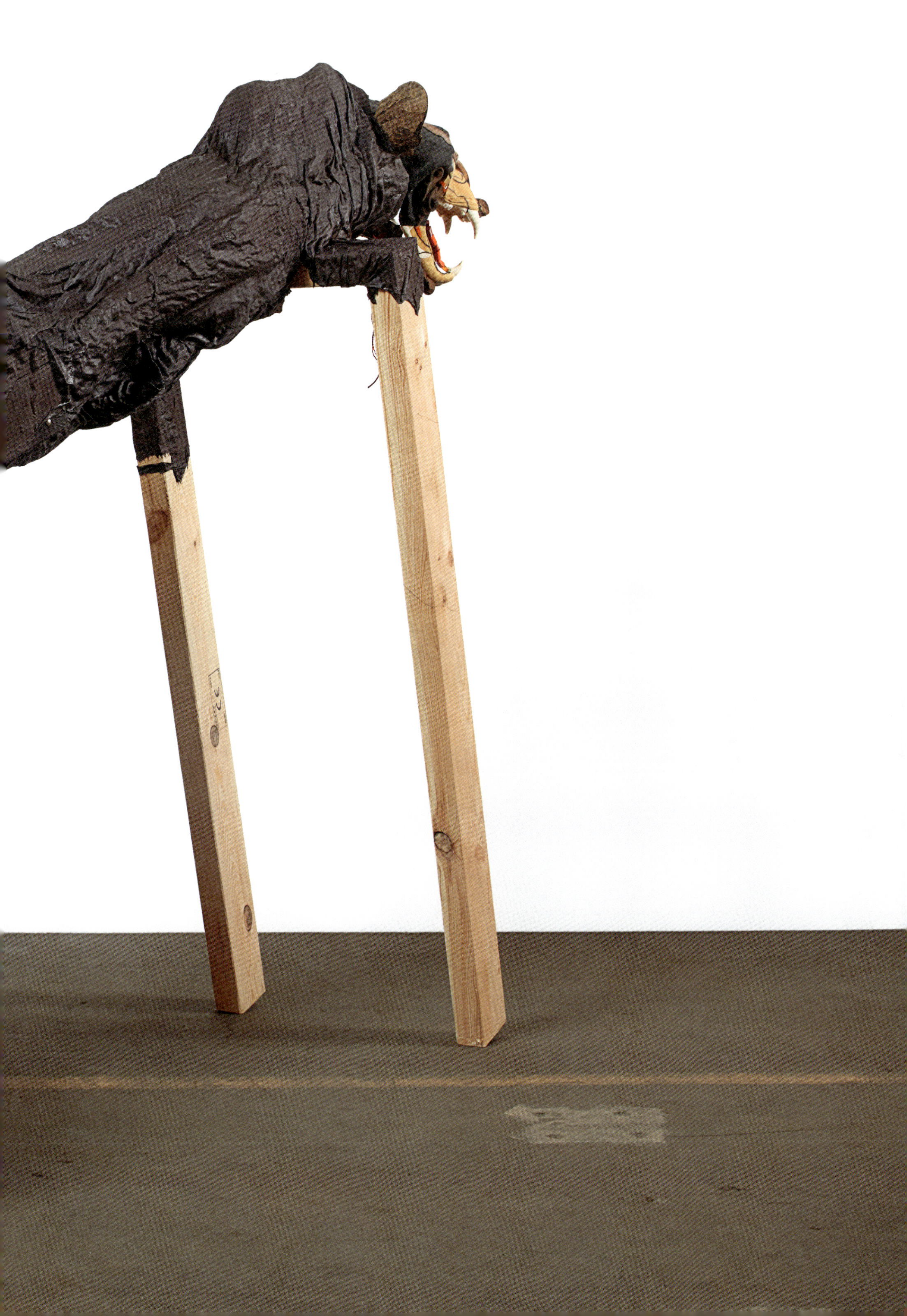

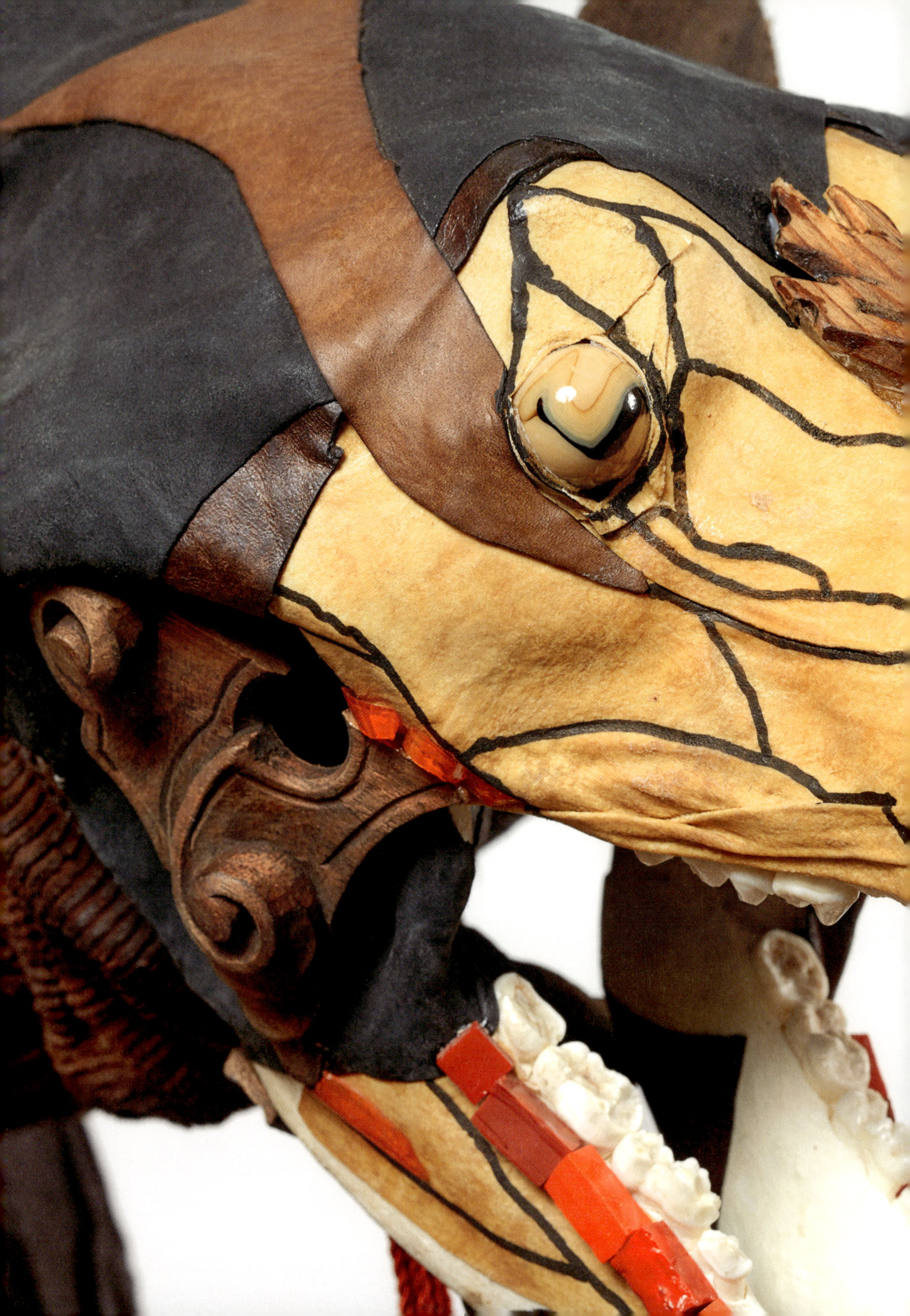

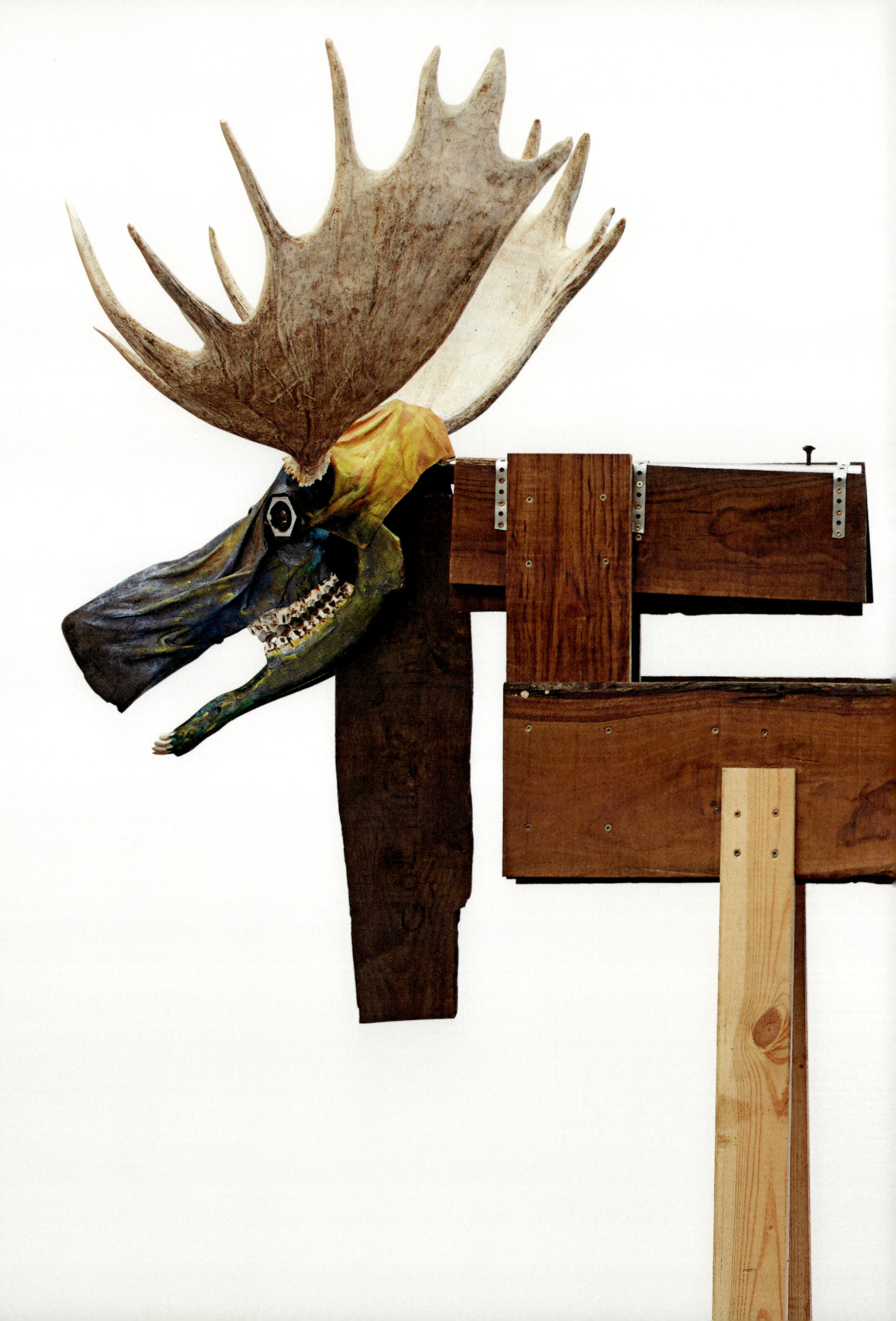

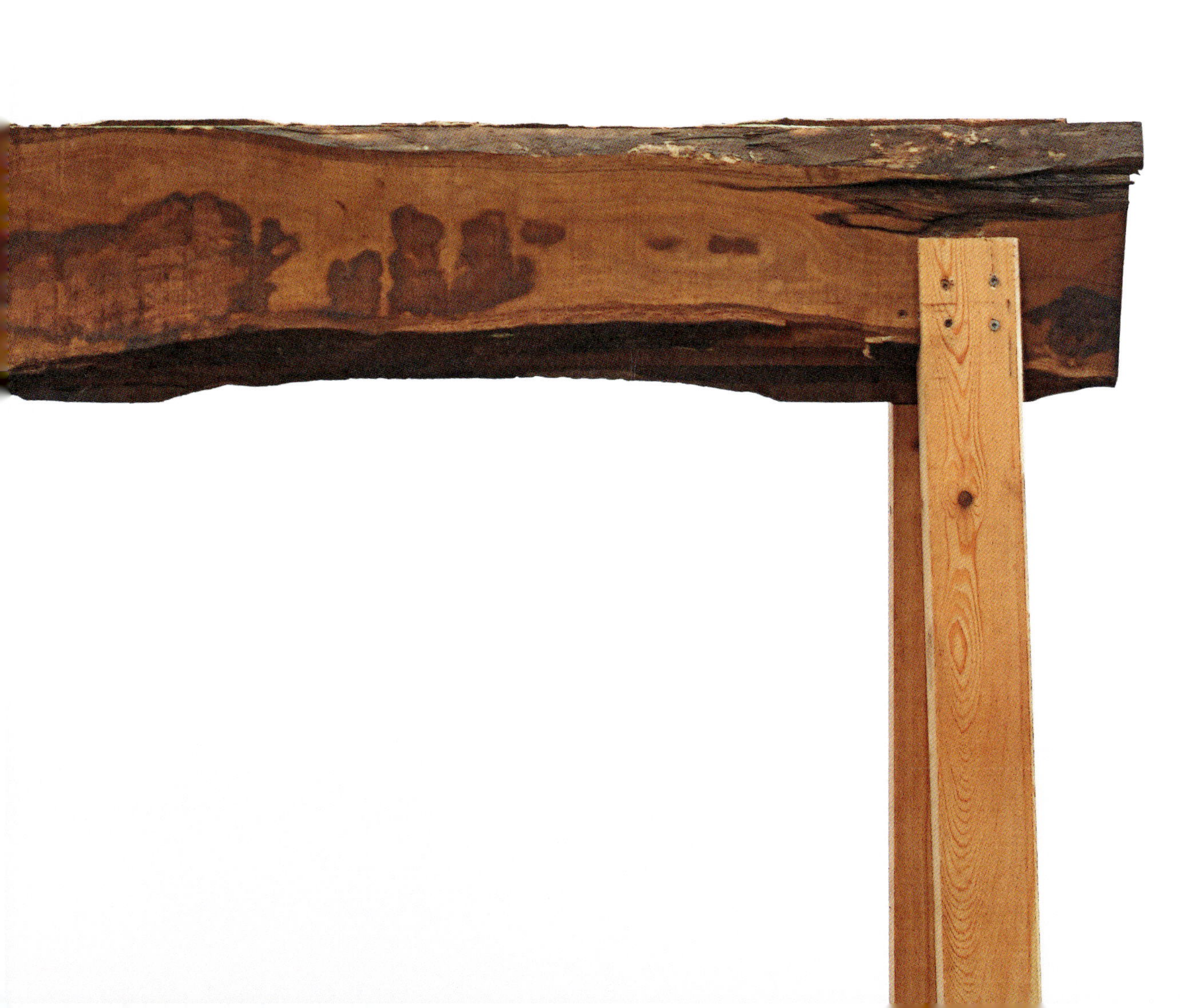

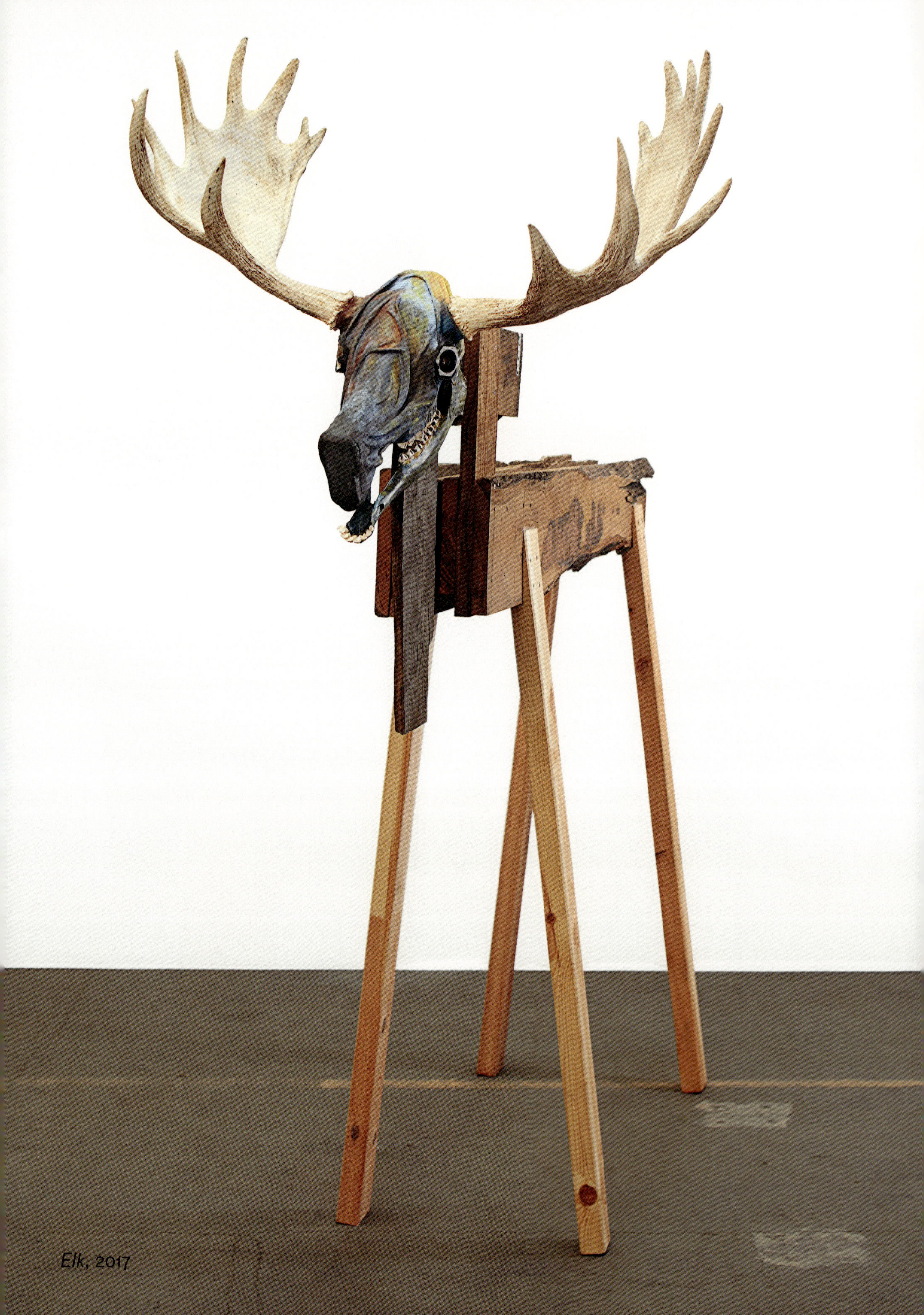

Elk, 2017

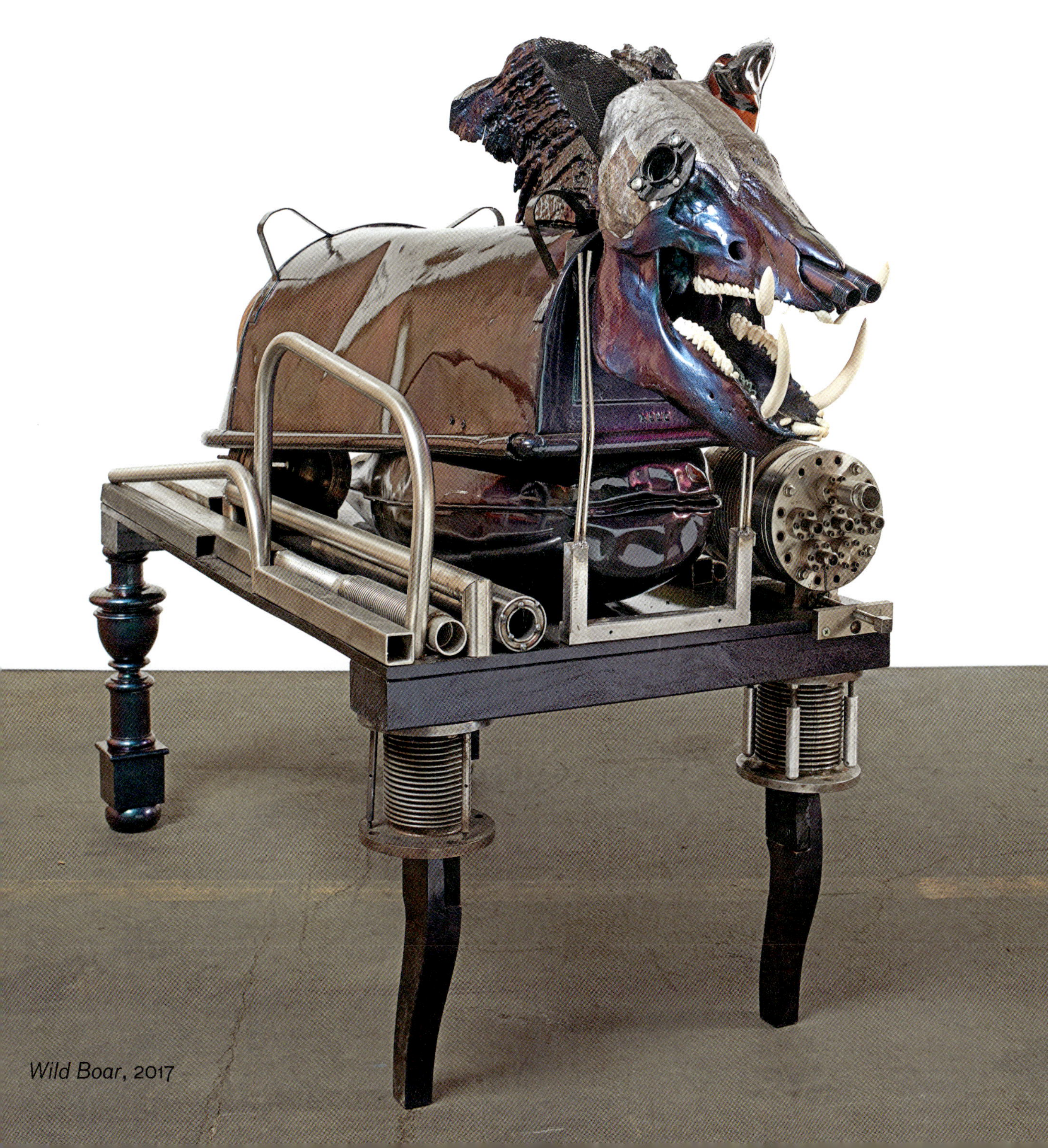

Wild Boar, 2017

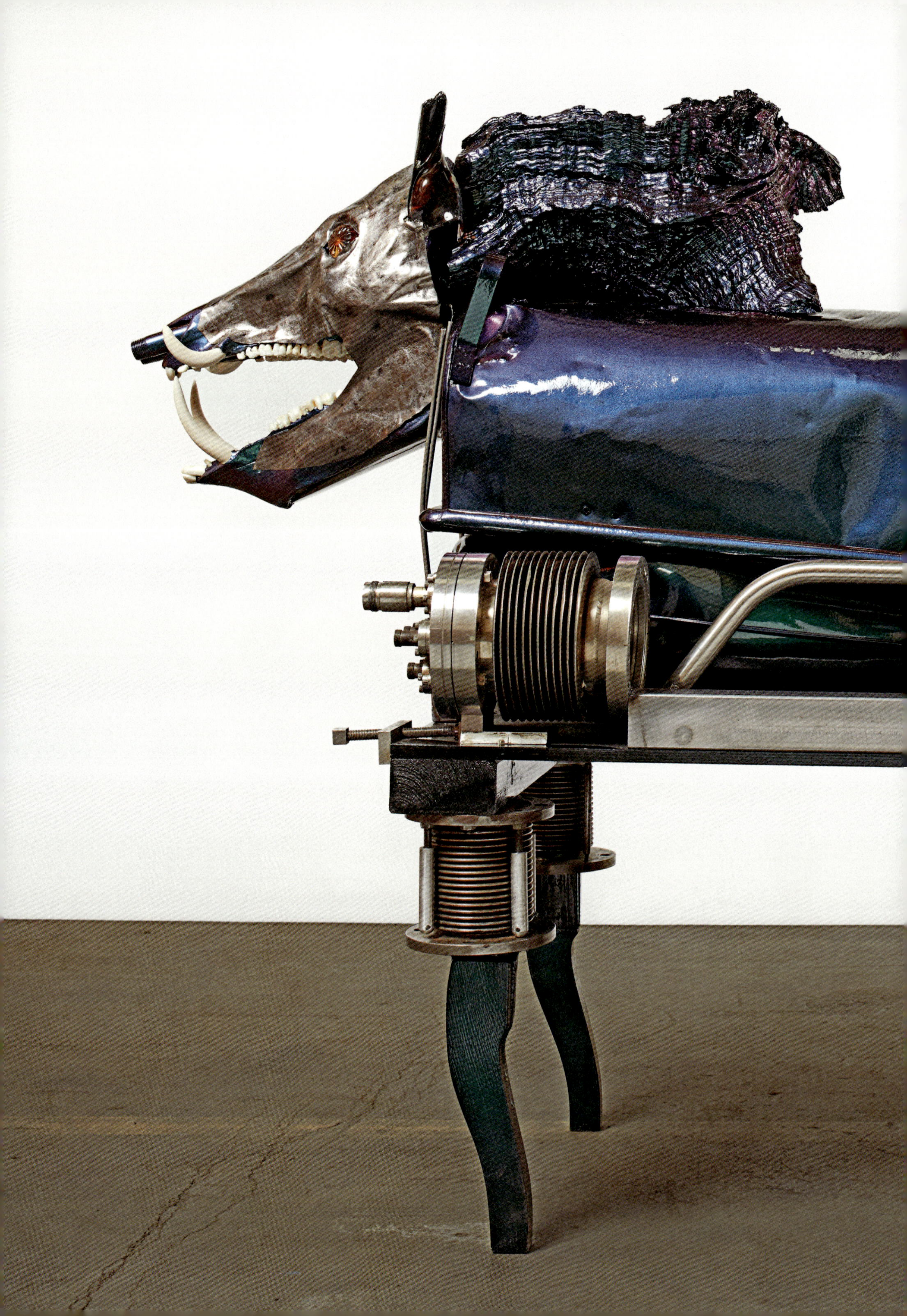

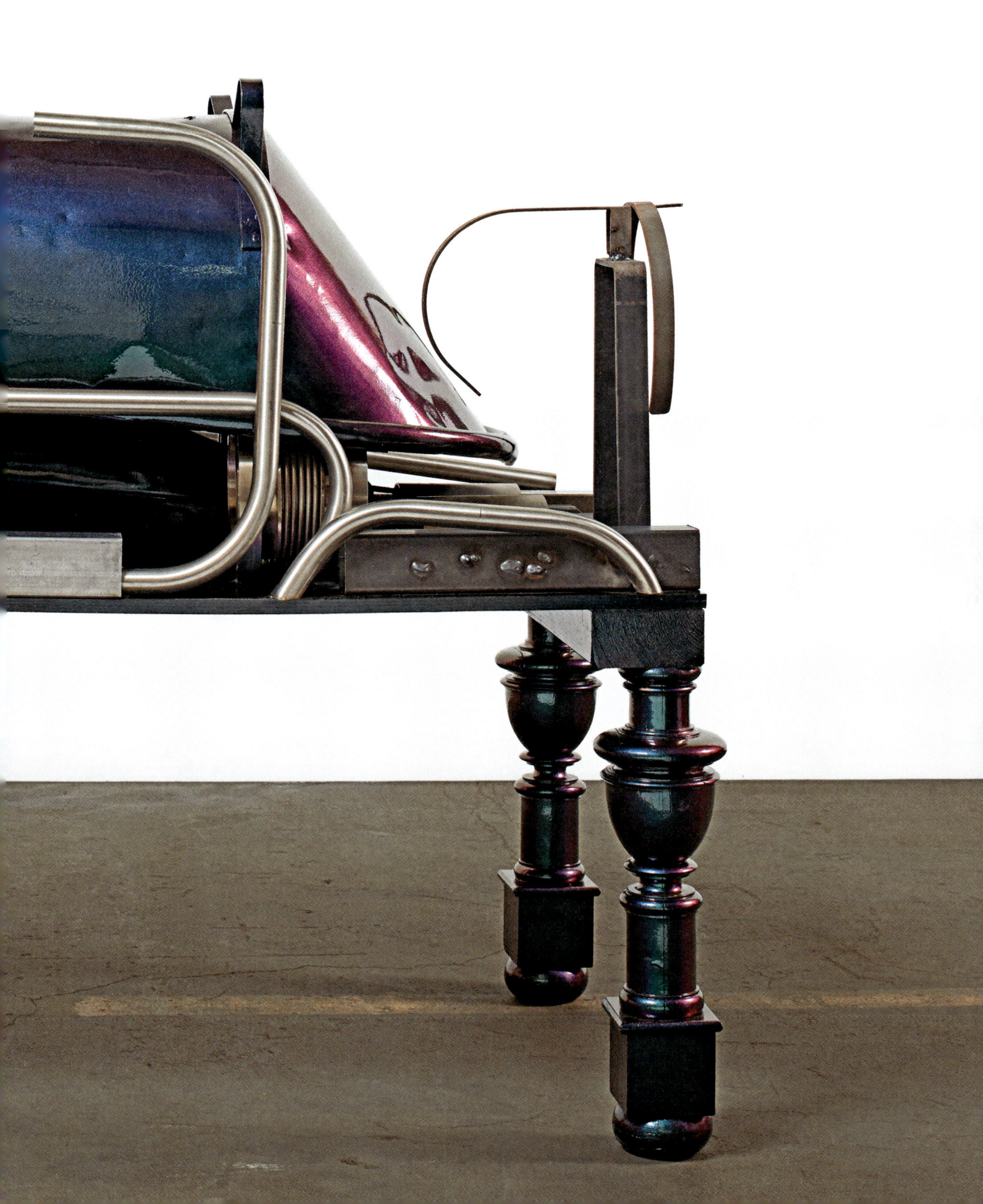

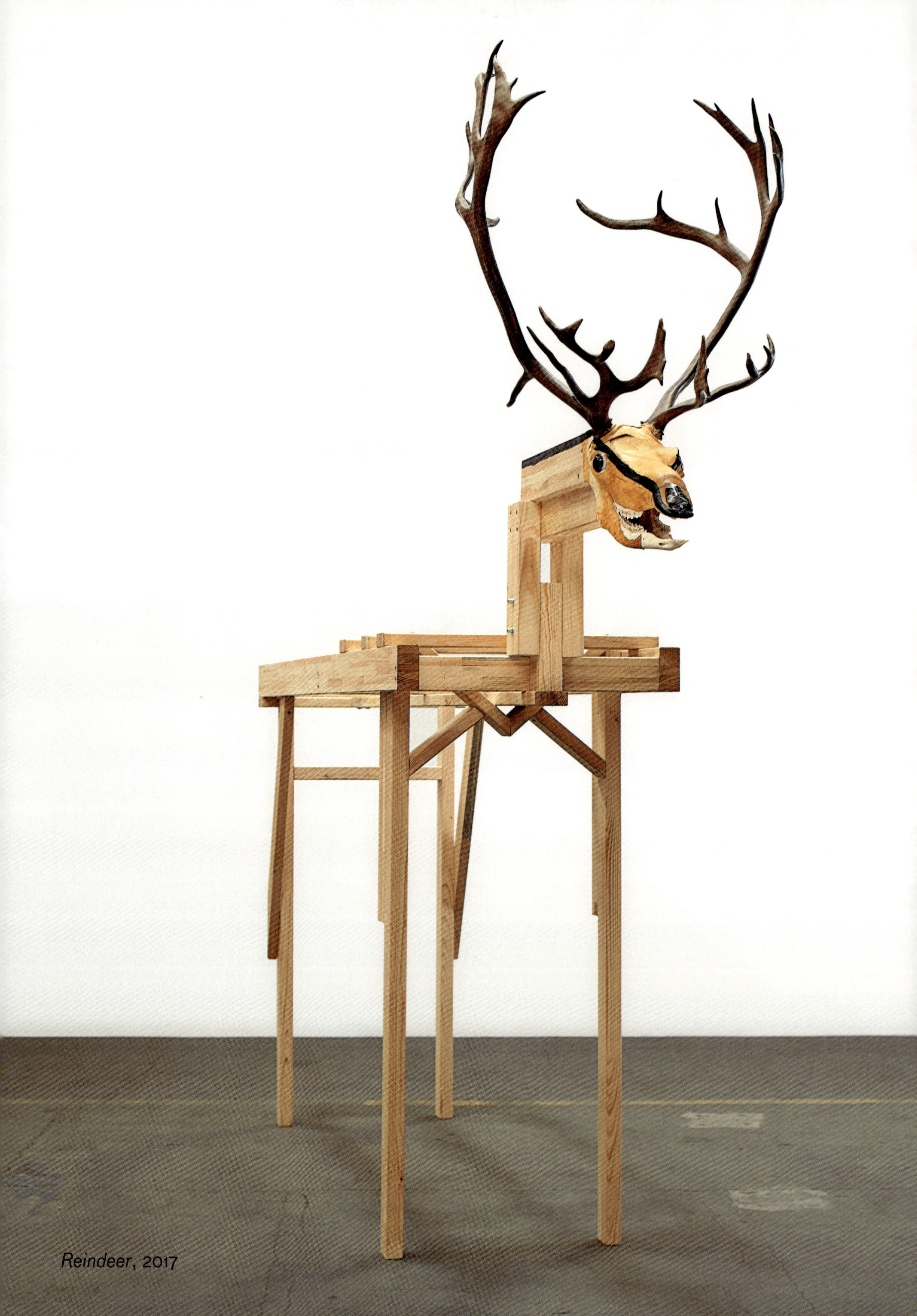

Reindeer, 2017

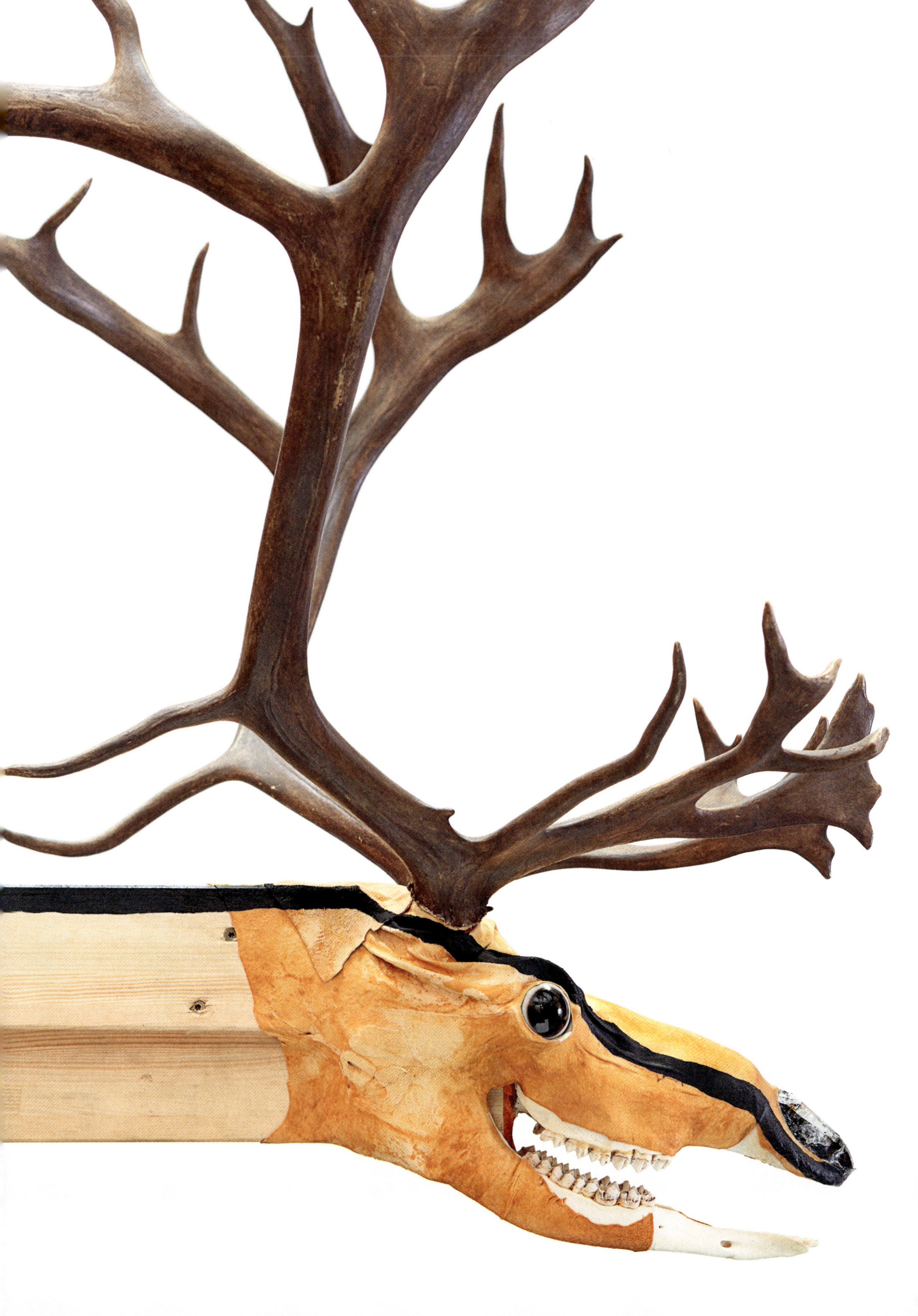

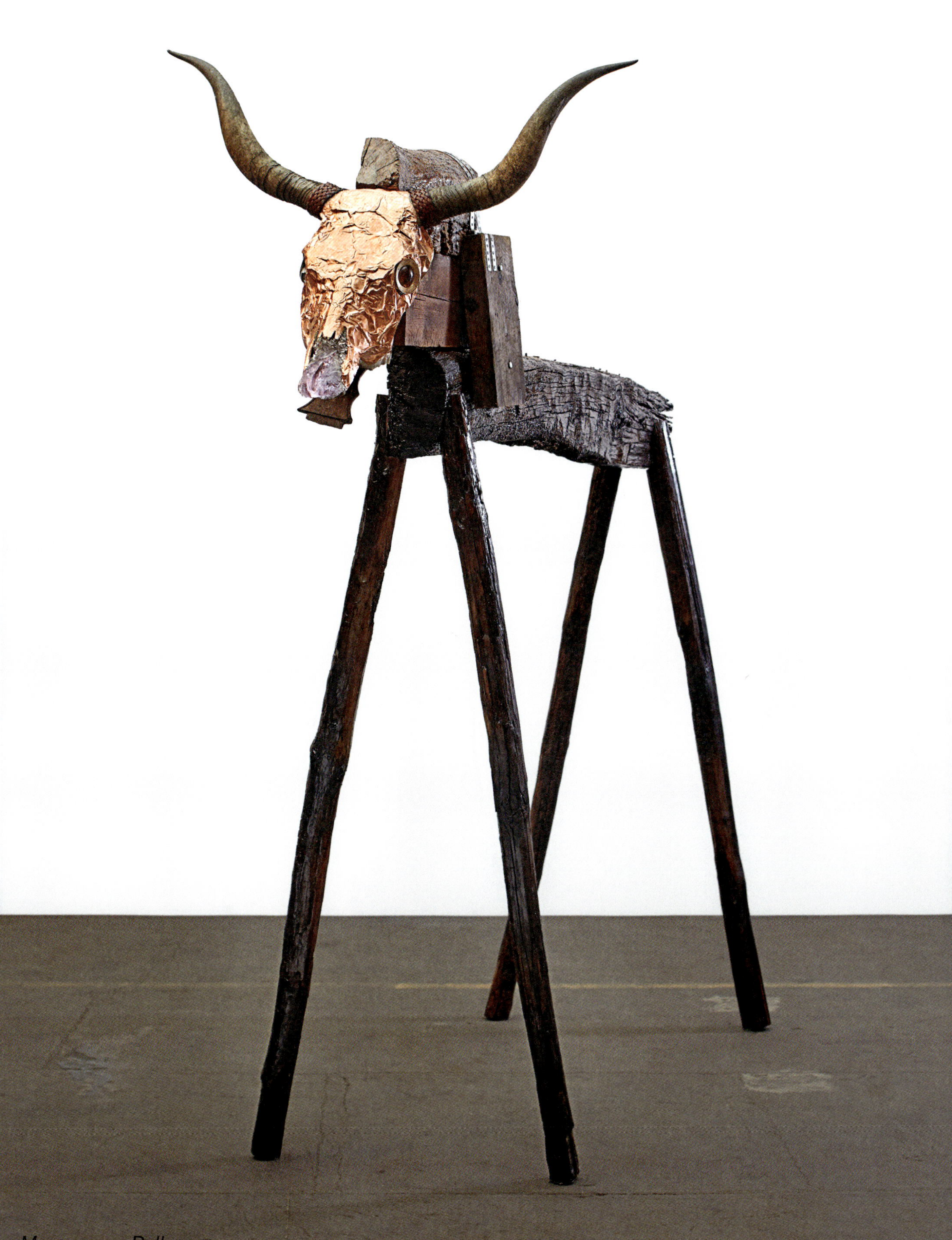

Maremmana Bull, 2017

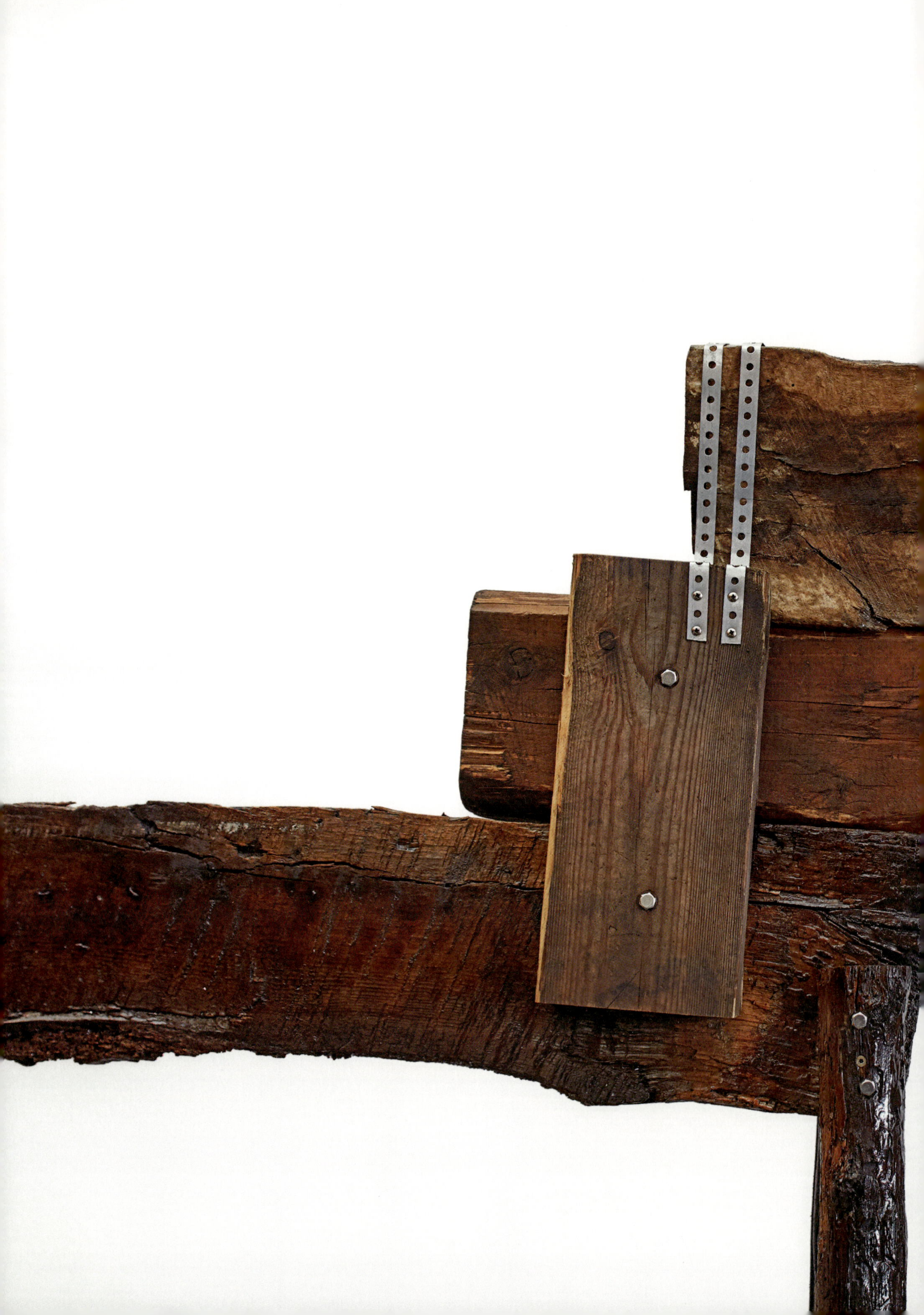

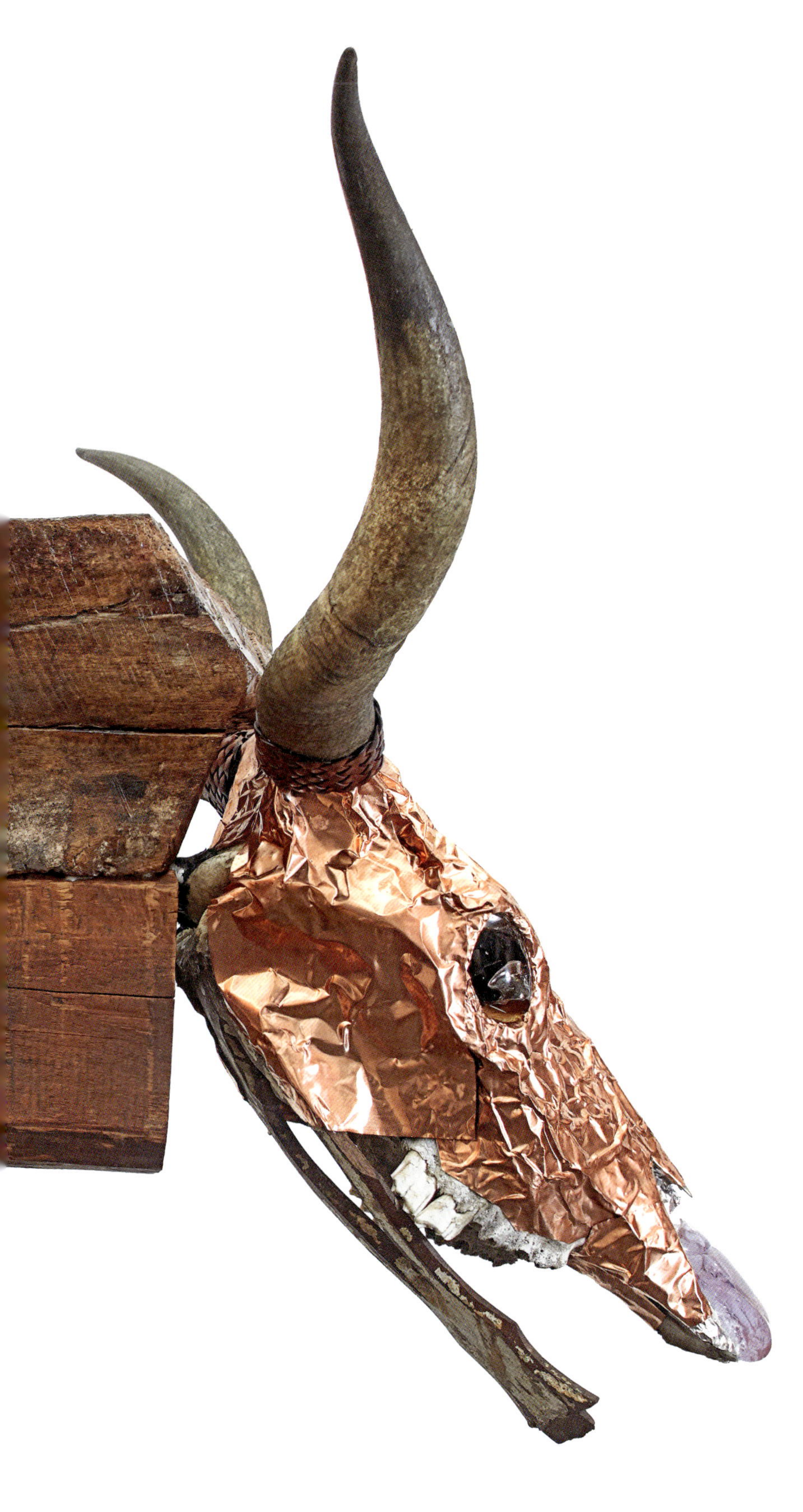

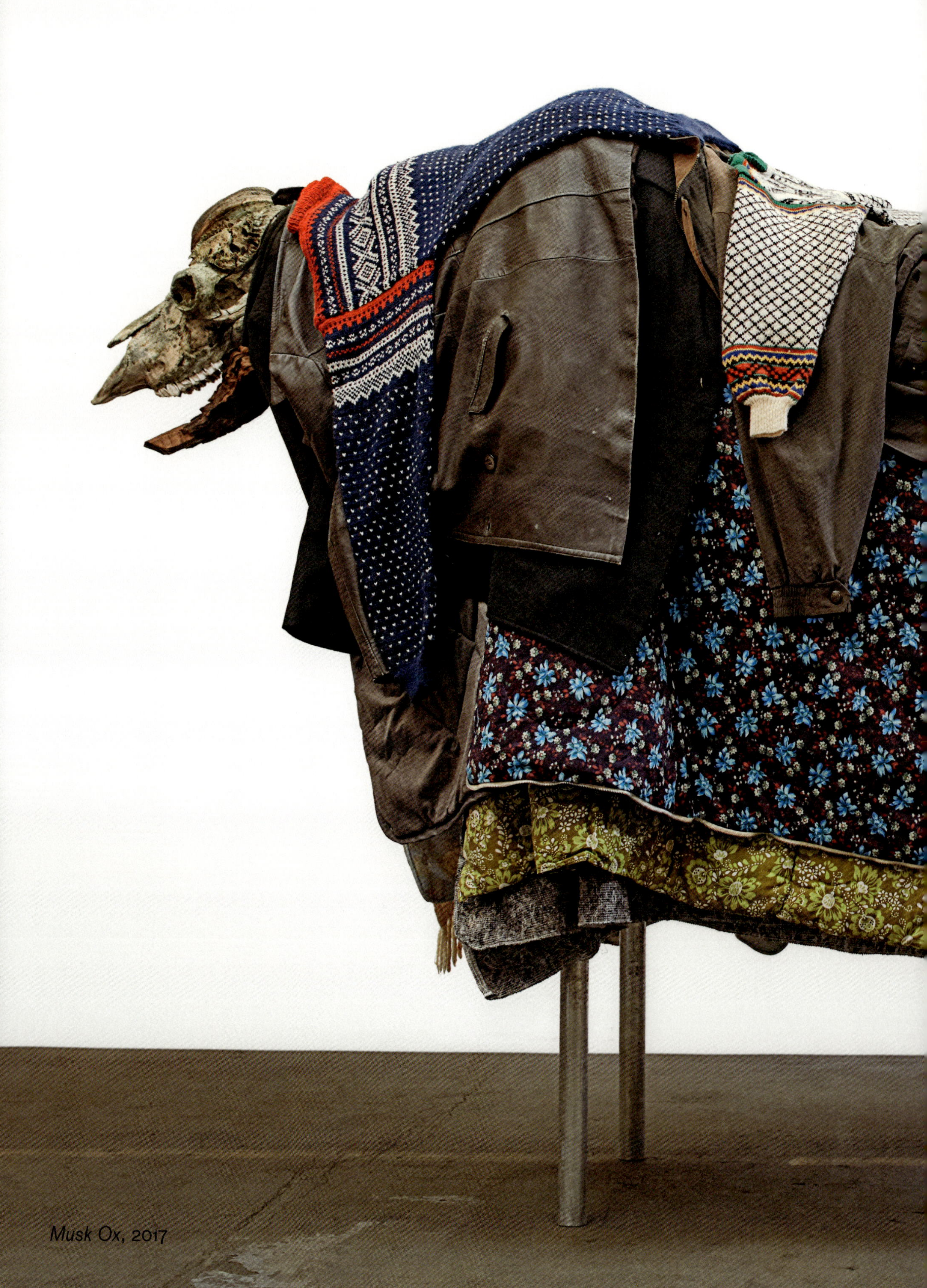

Musk Ox, 2017

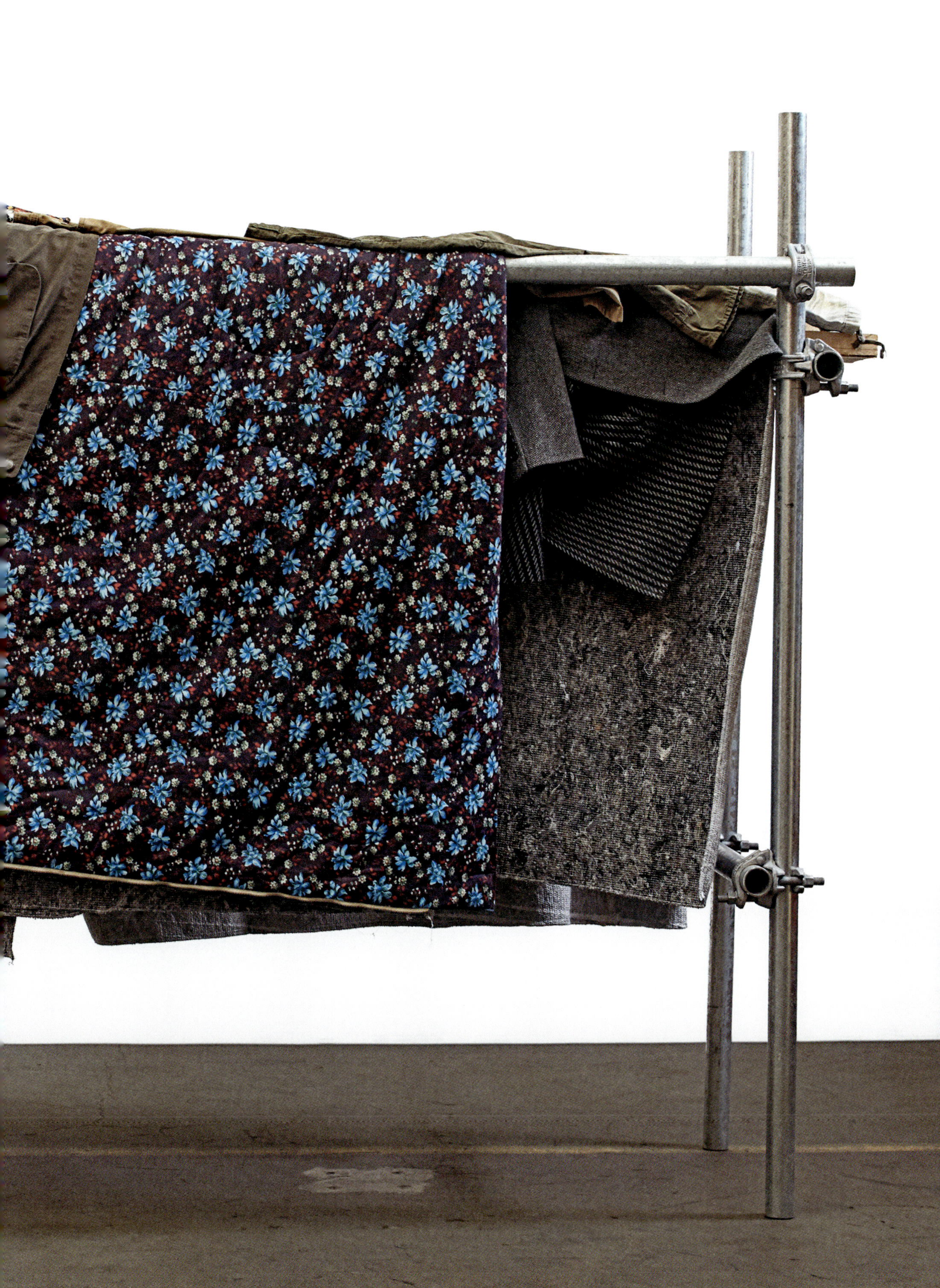

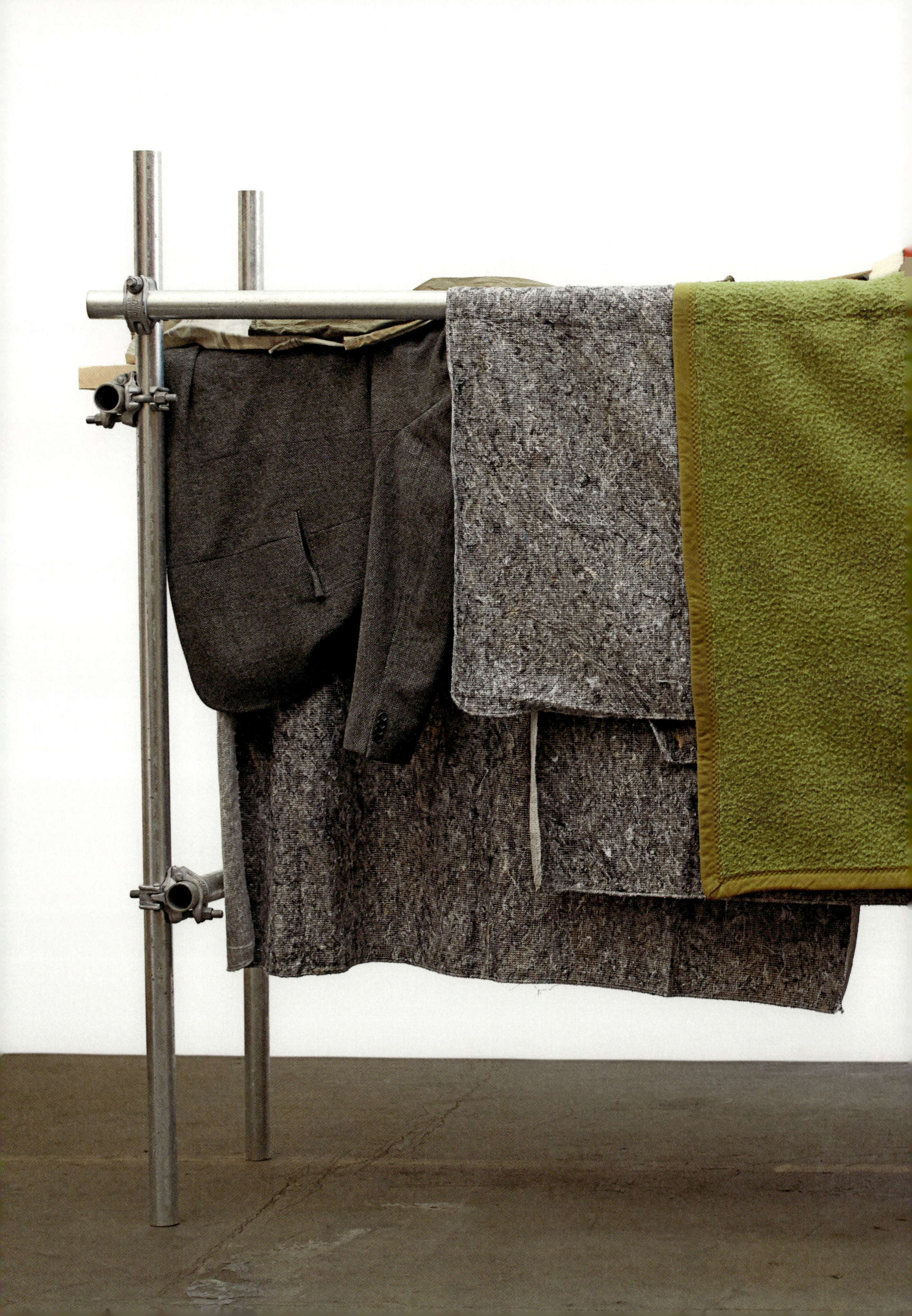

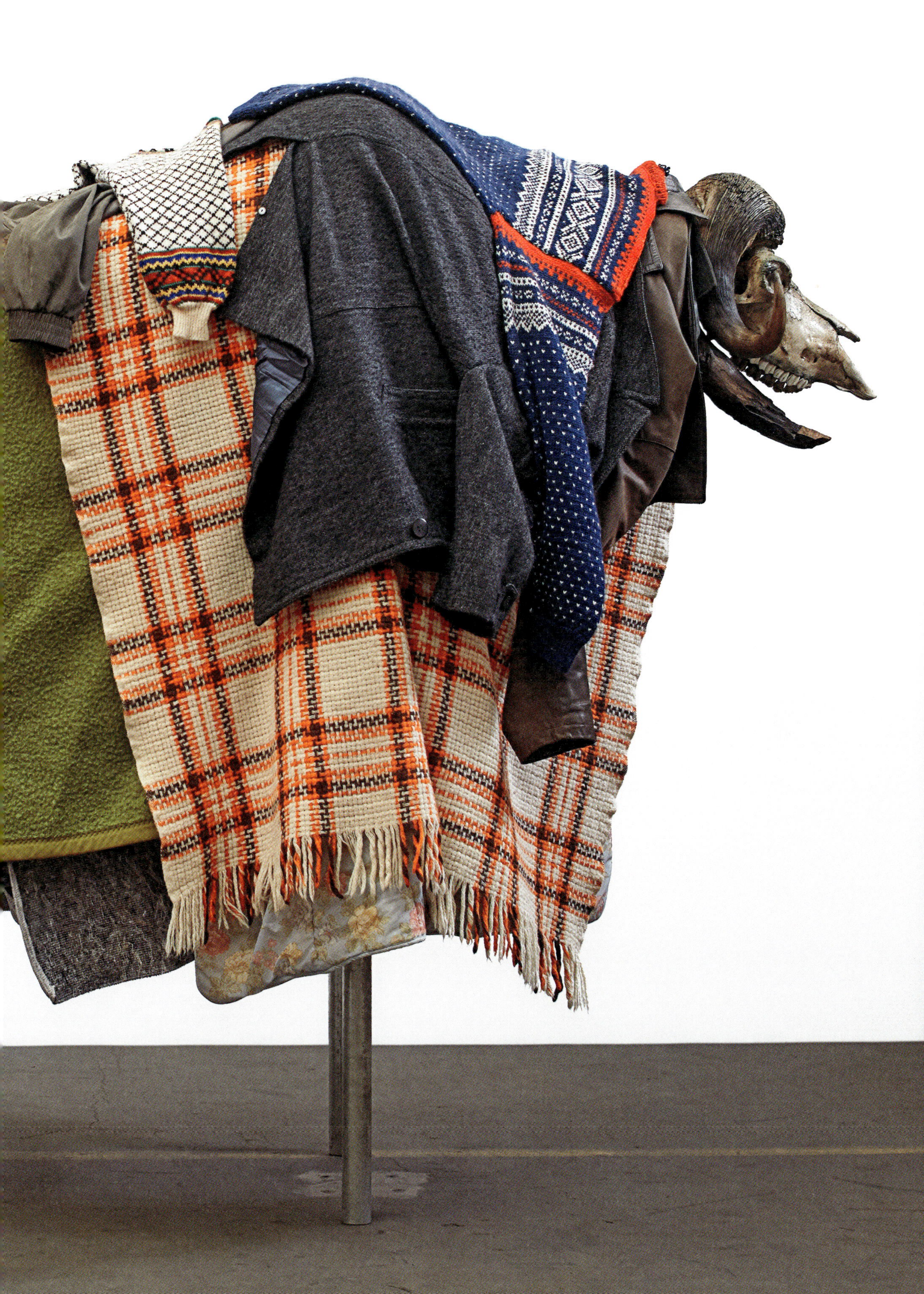

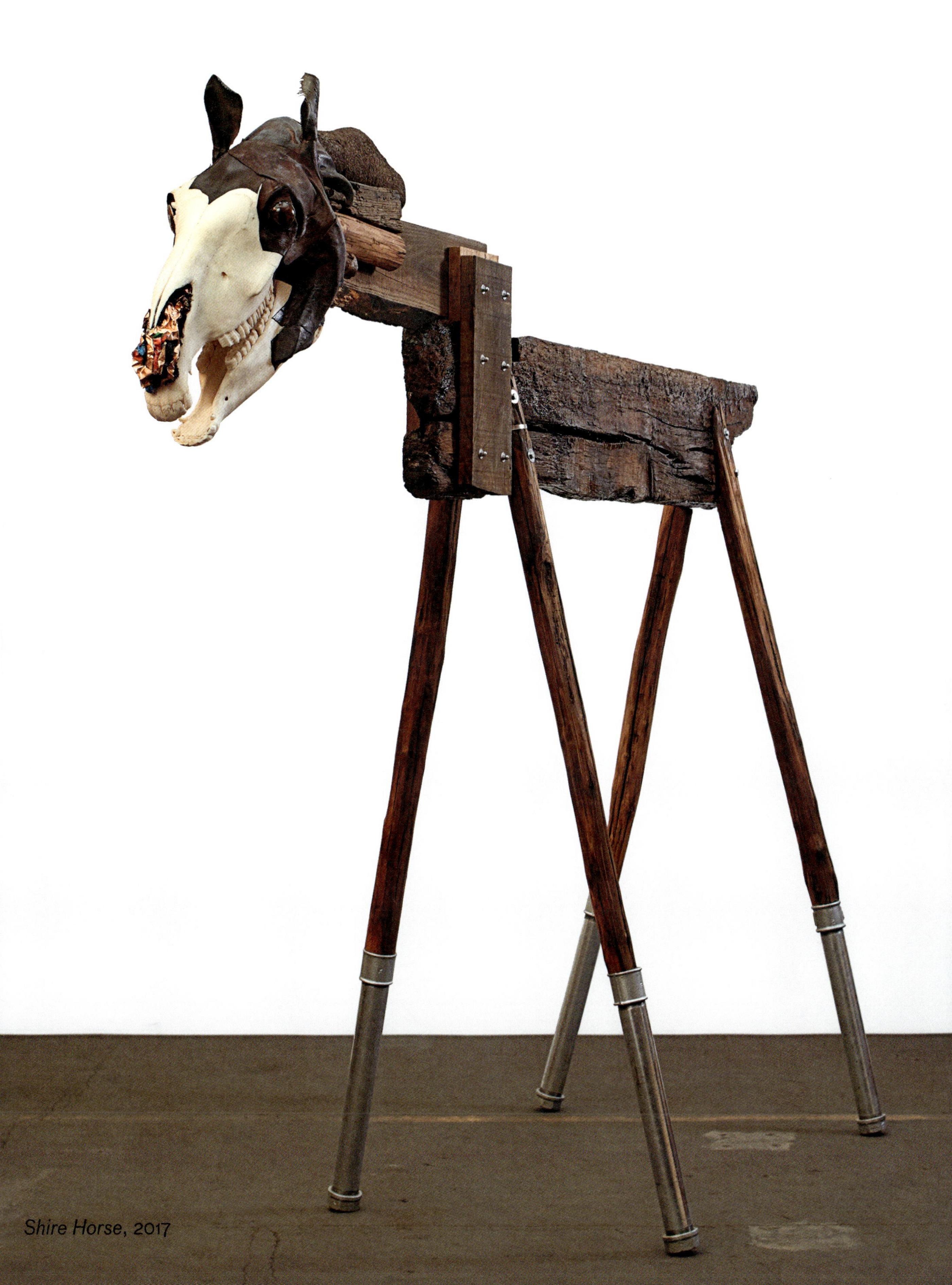

Shire Horse, 2017

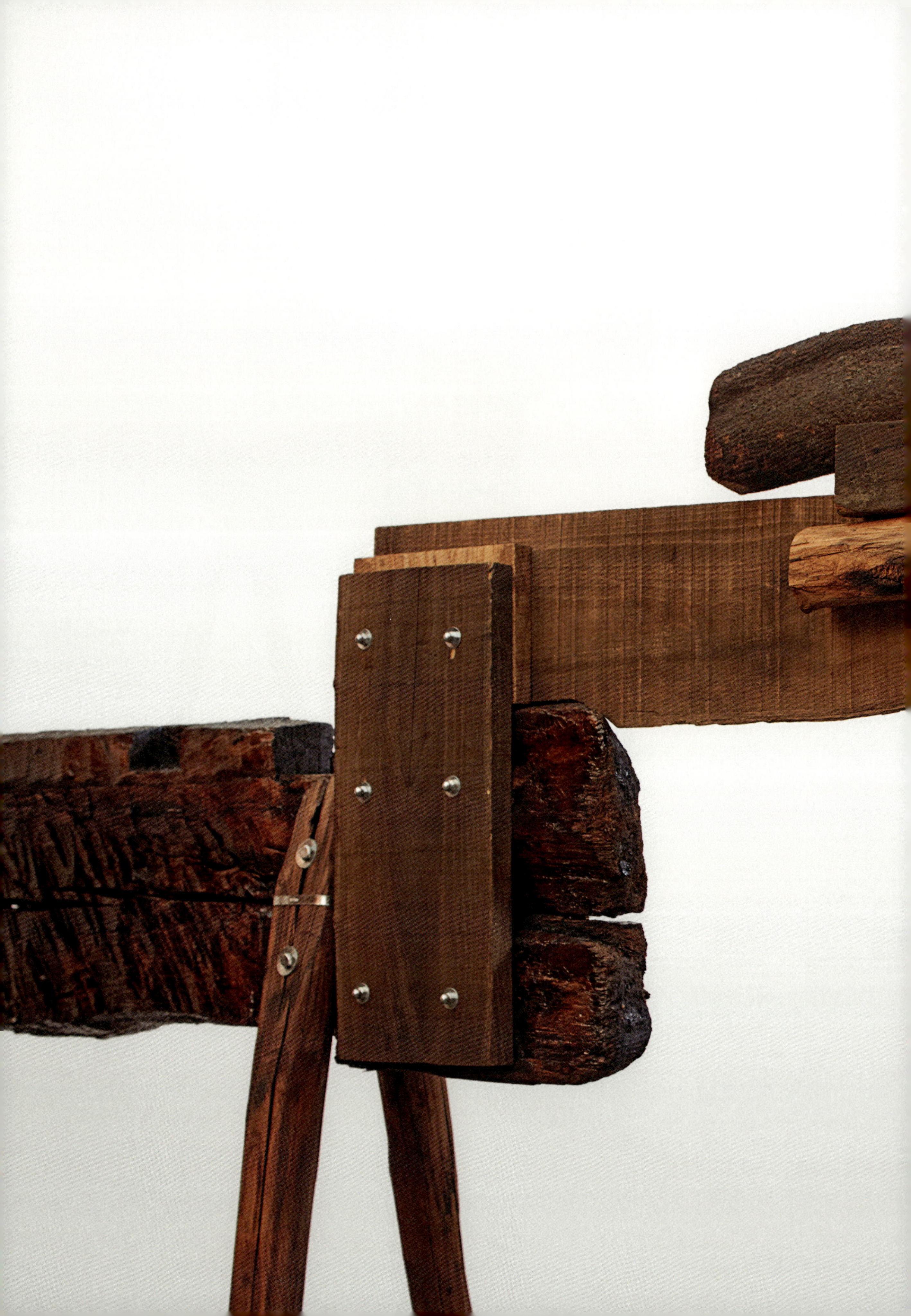

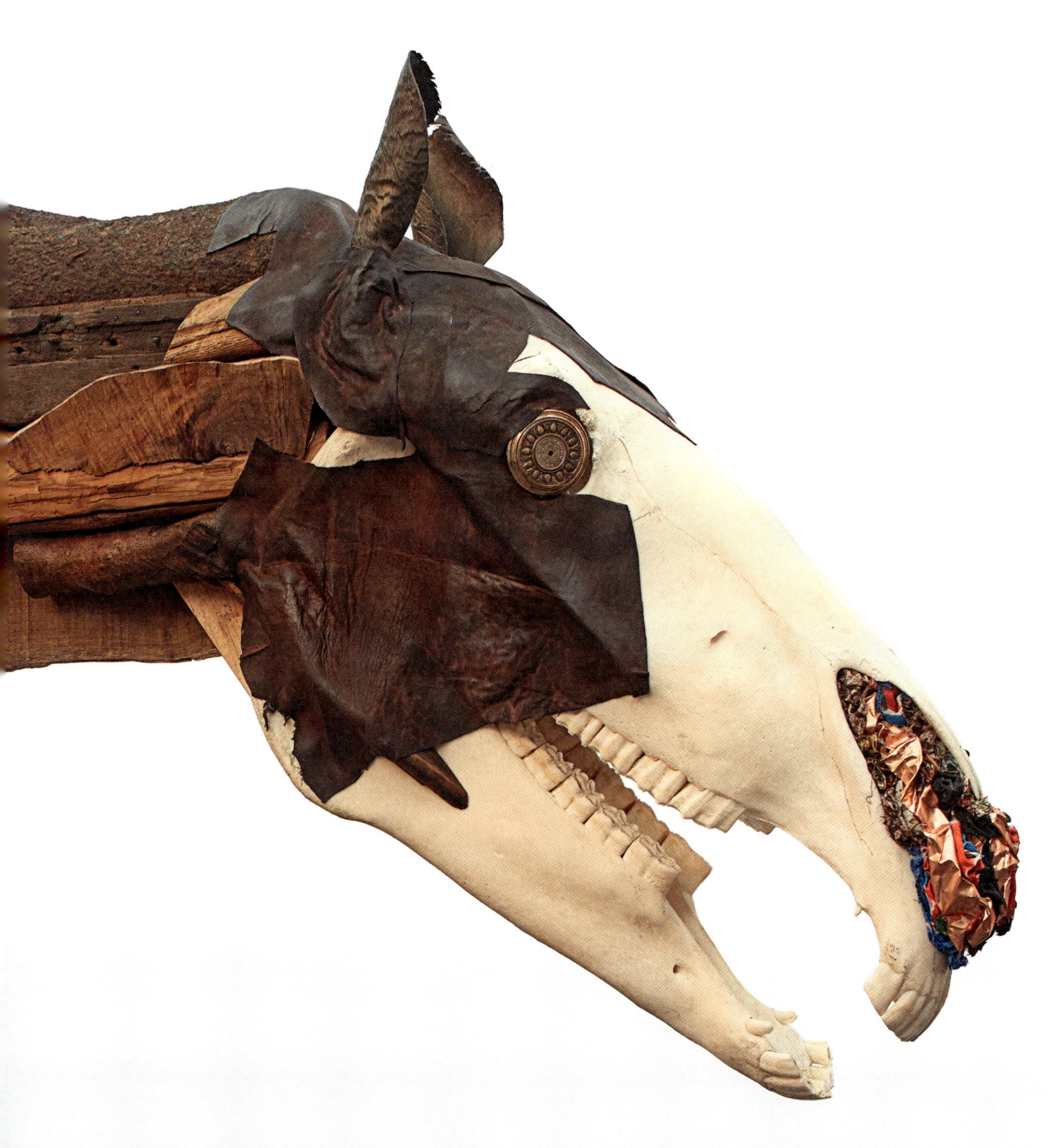

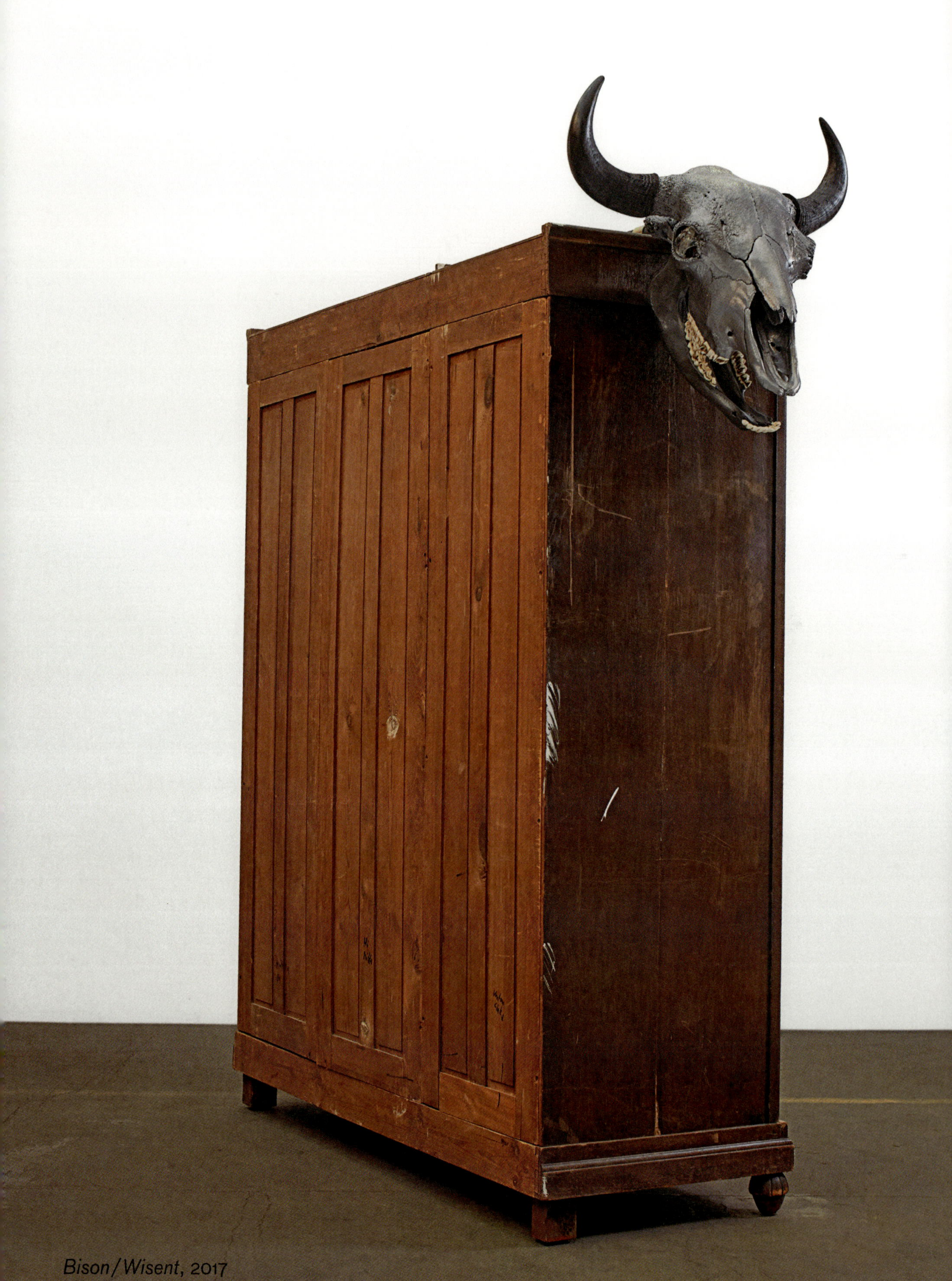

Bison / Wisent, 2017

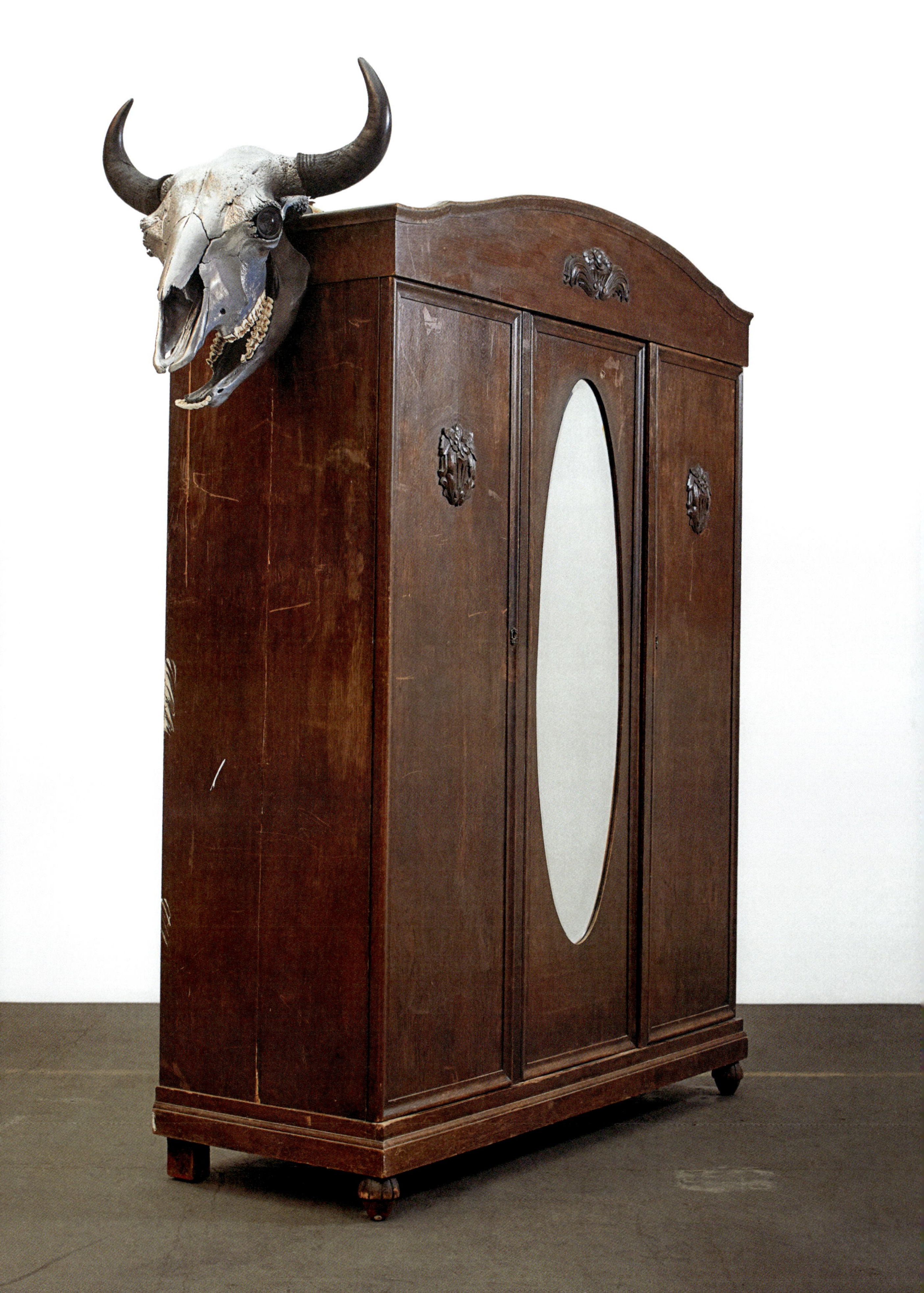

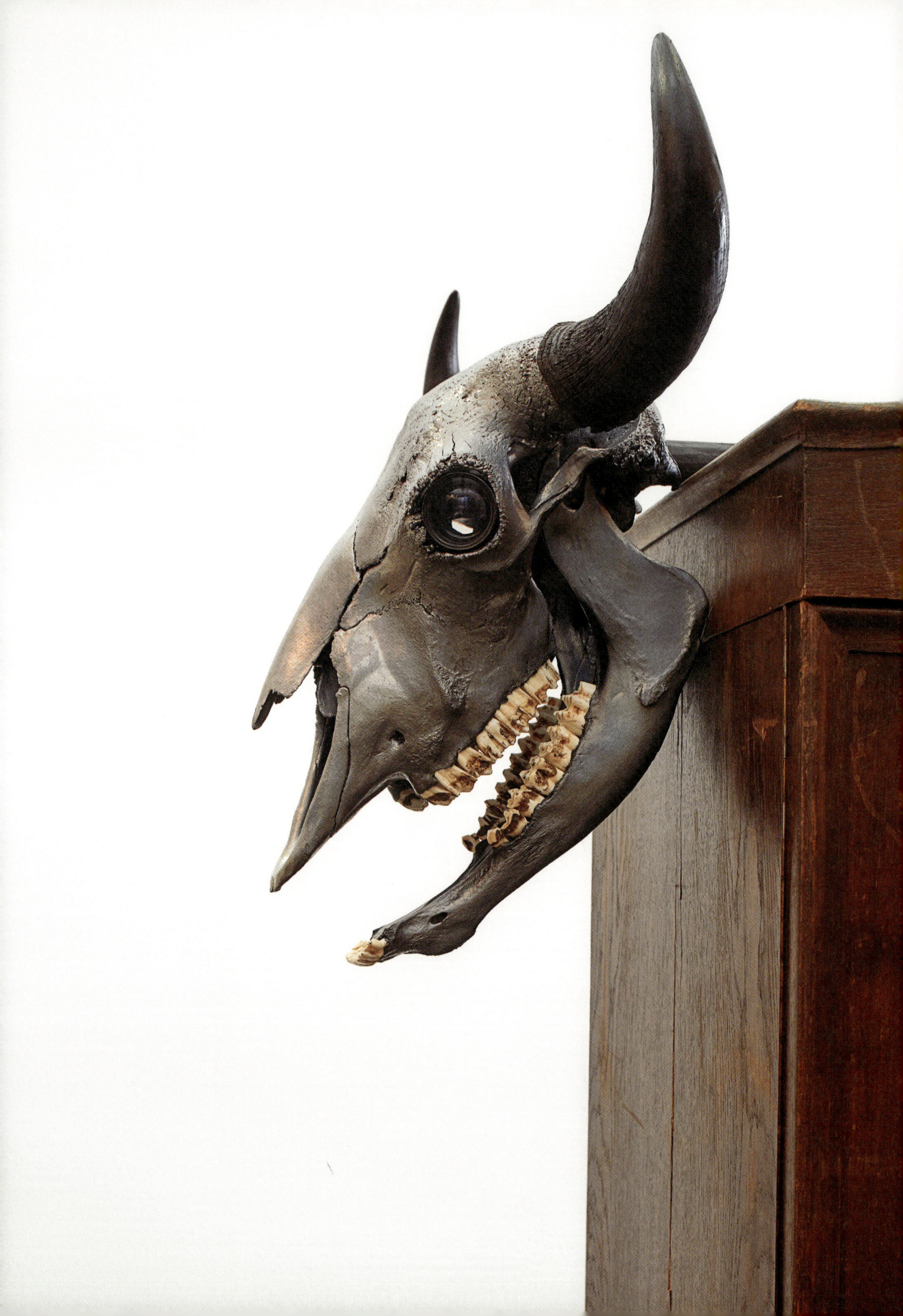

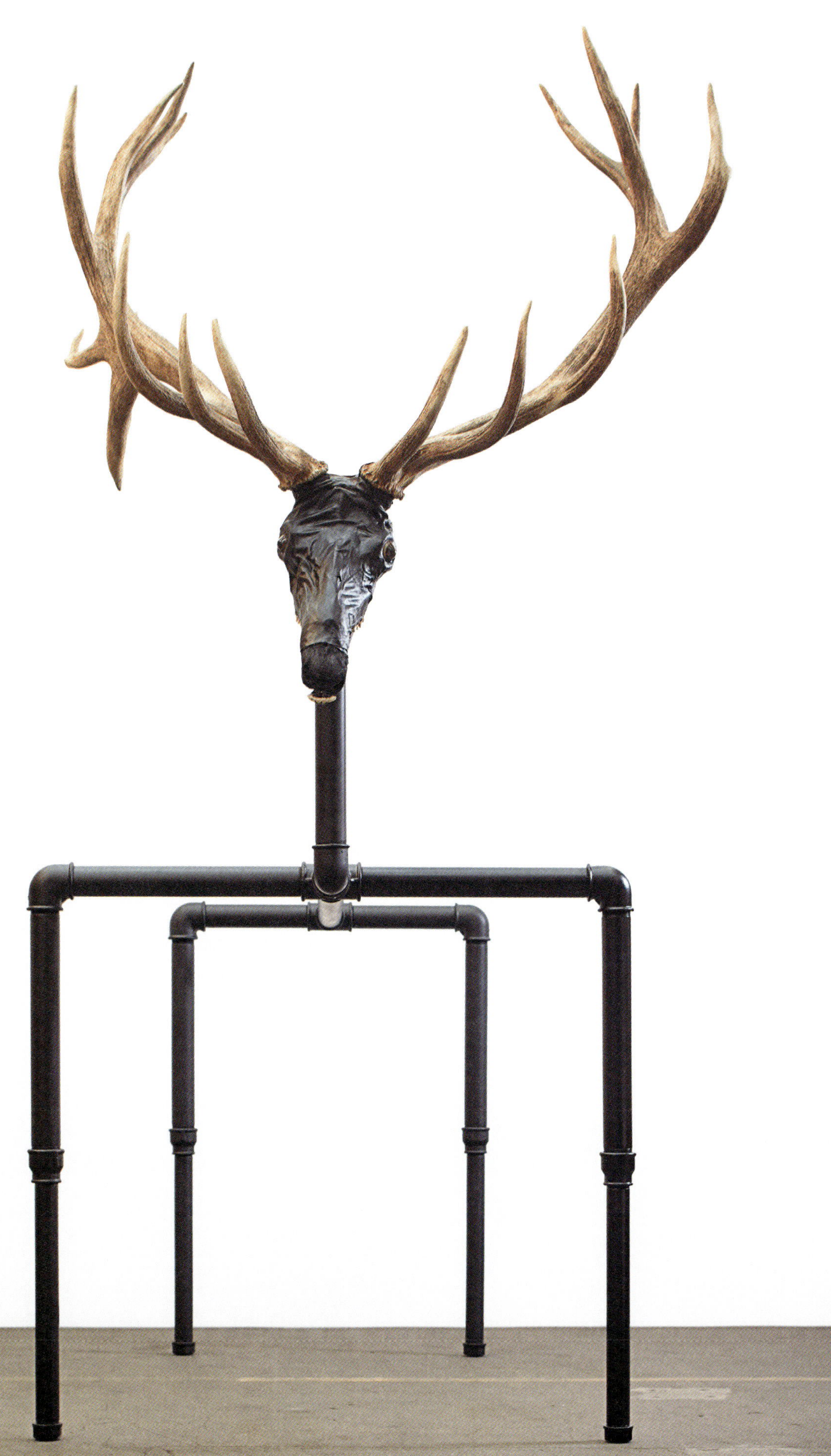

Red Deer, 2017

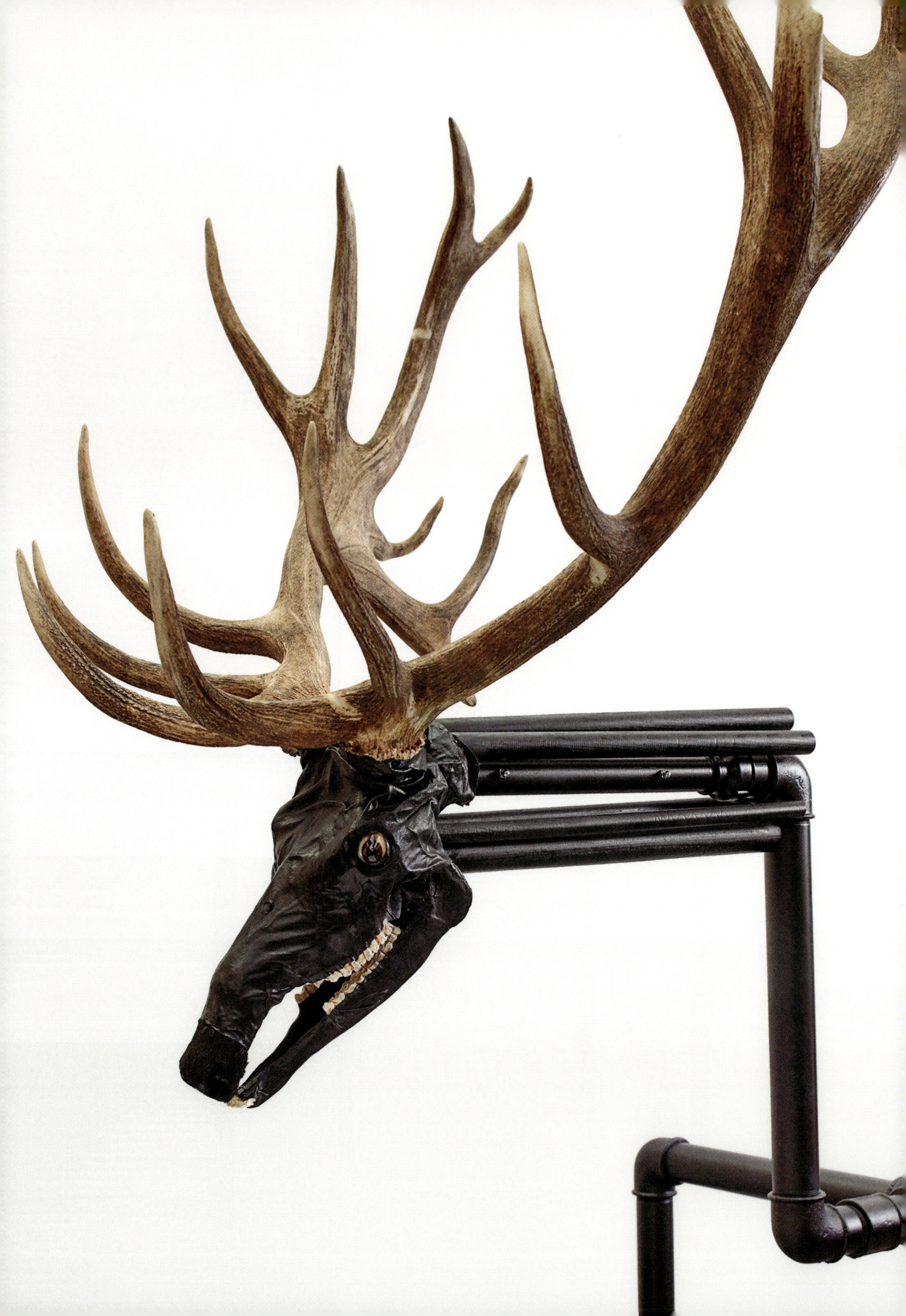

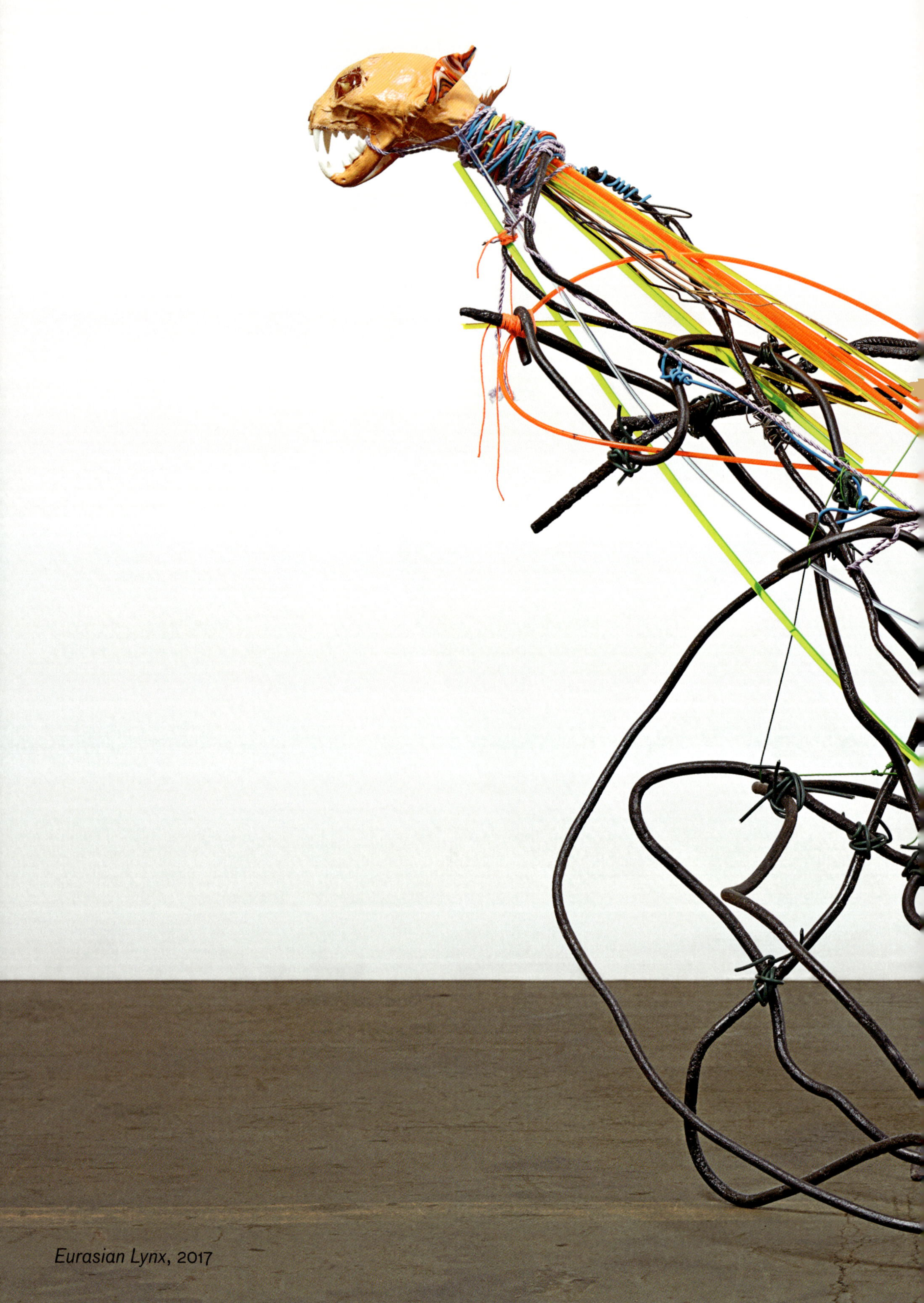

Eurasian Lynx, 2017

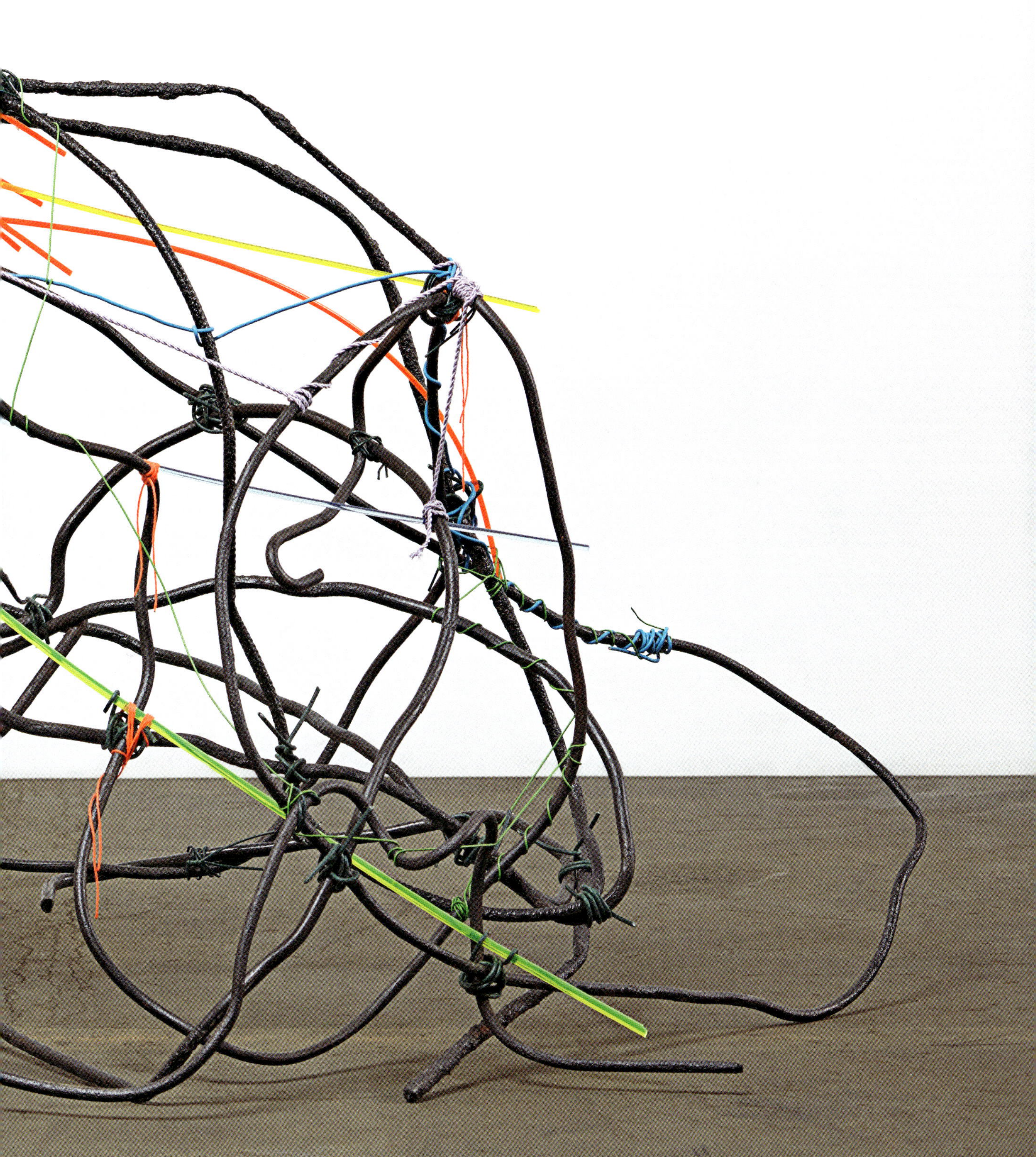

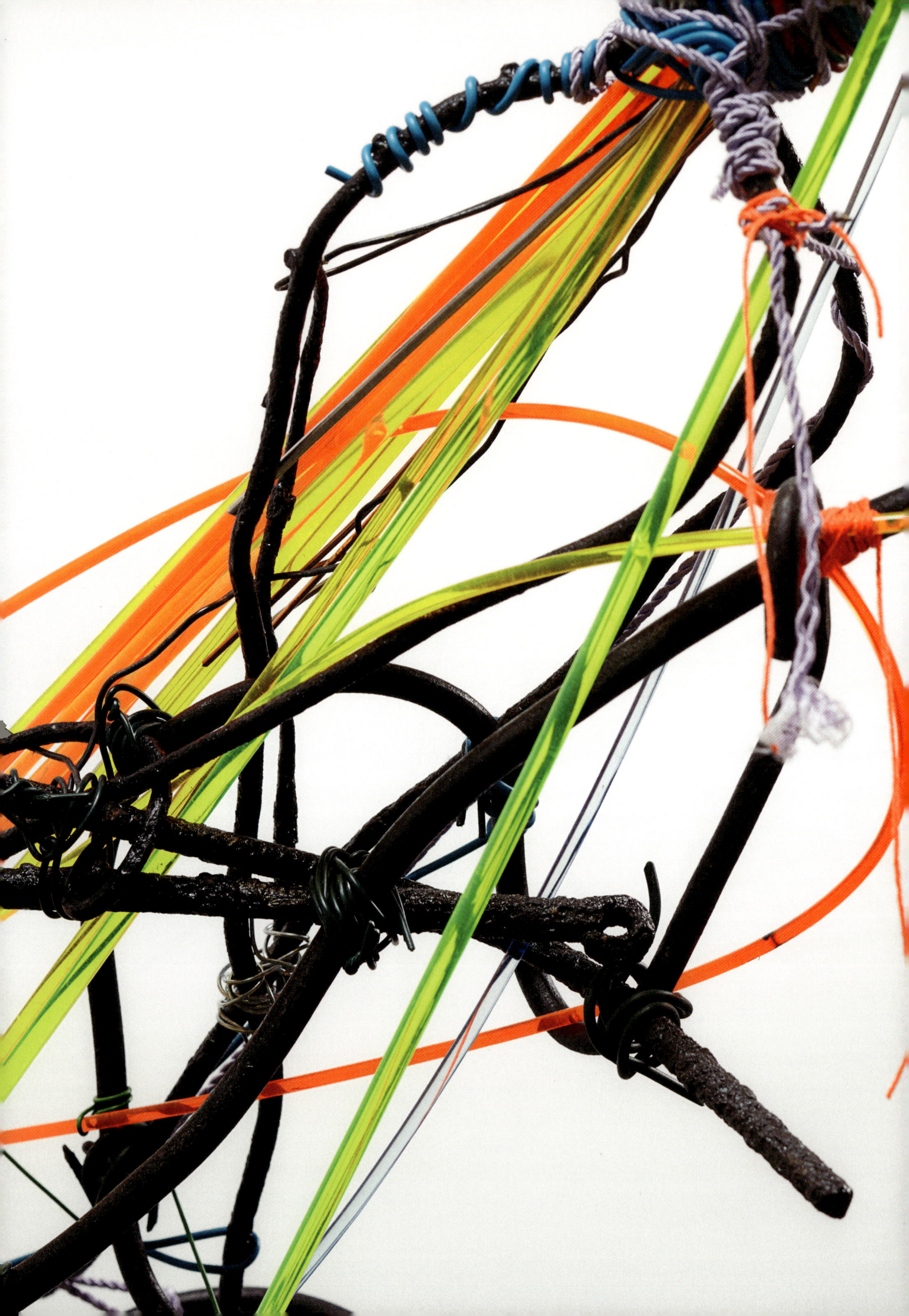

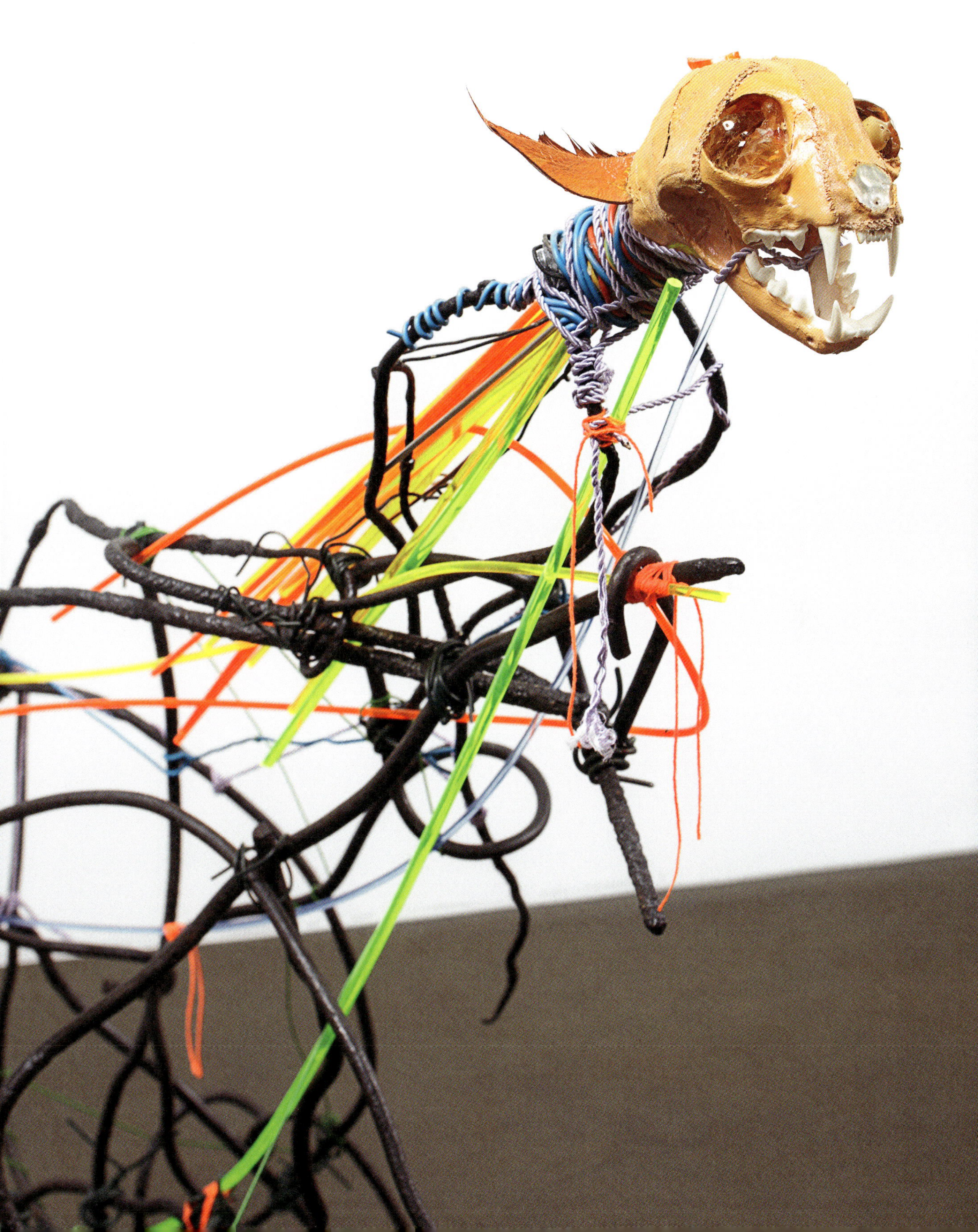

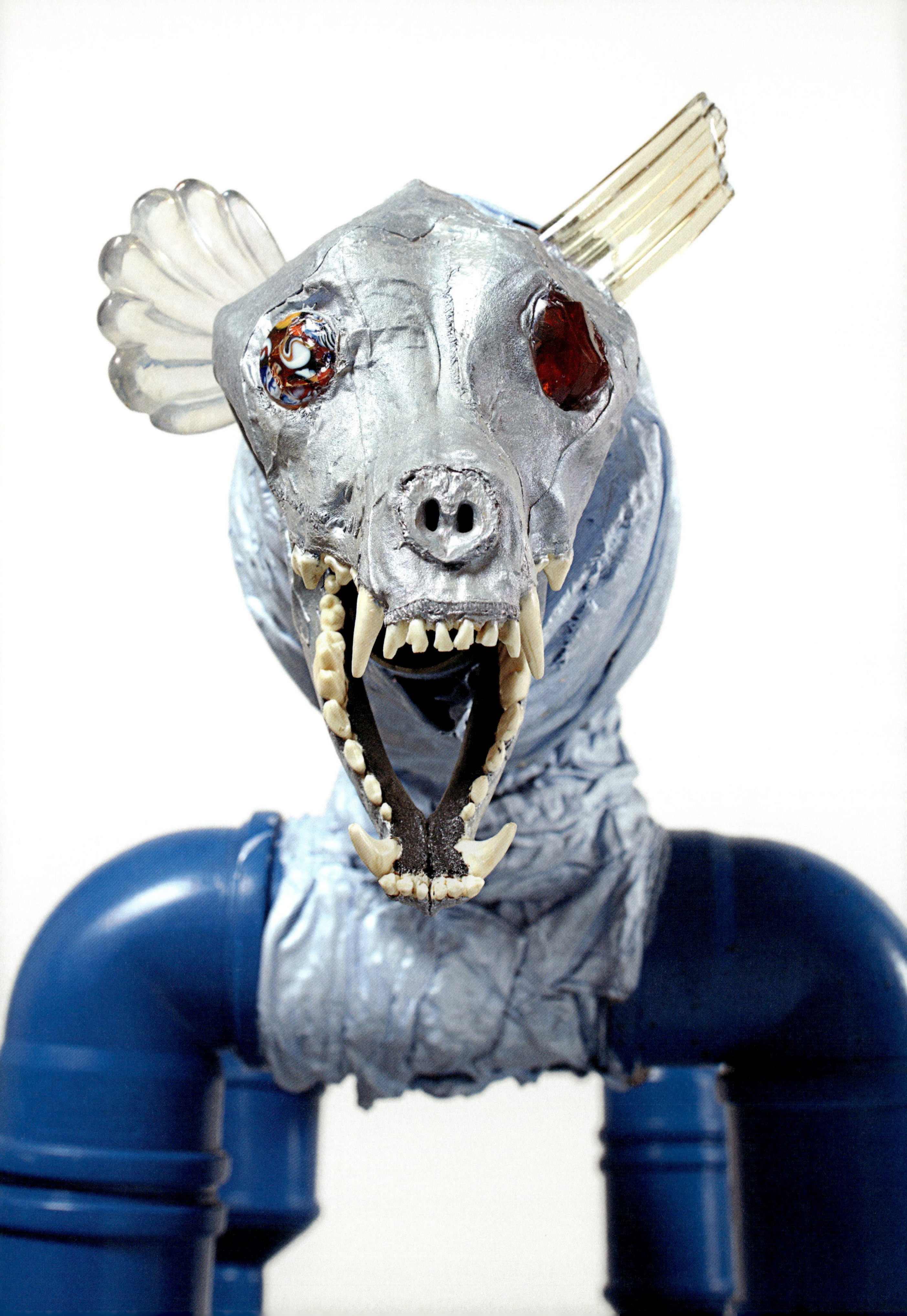

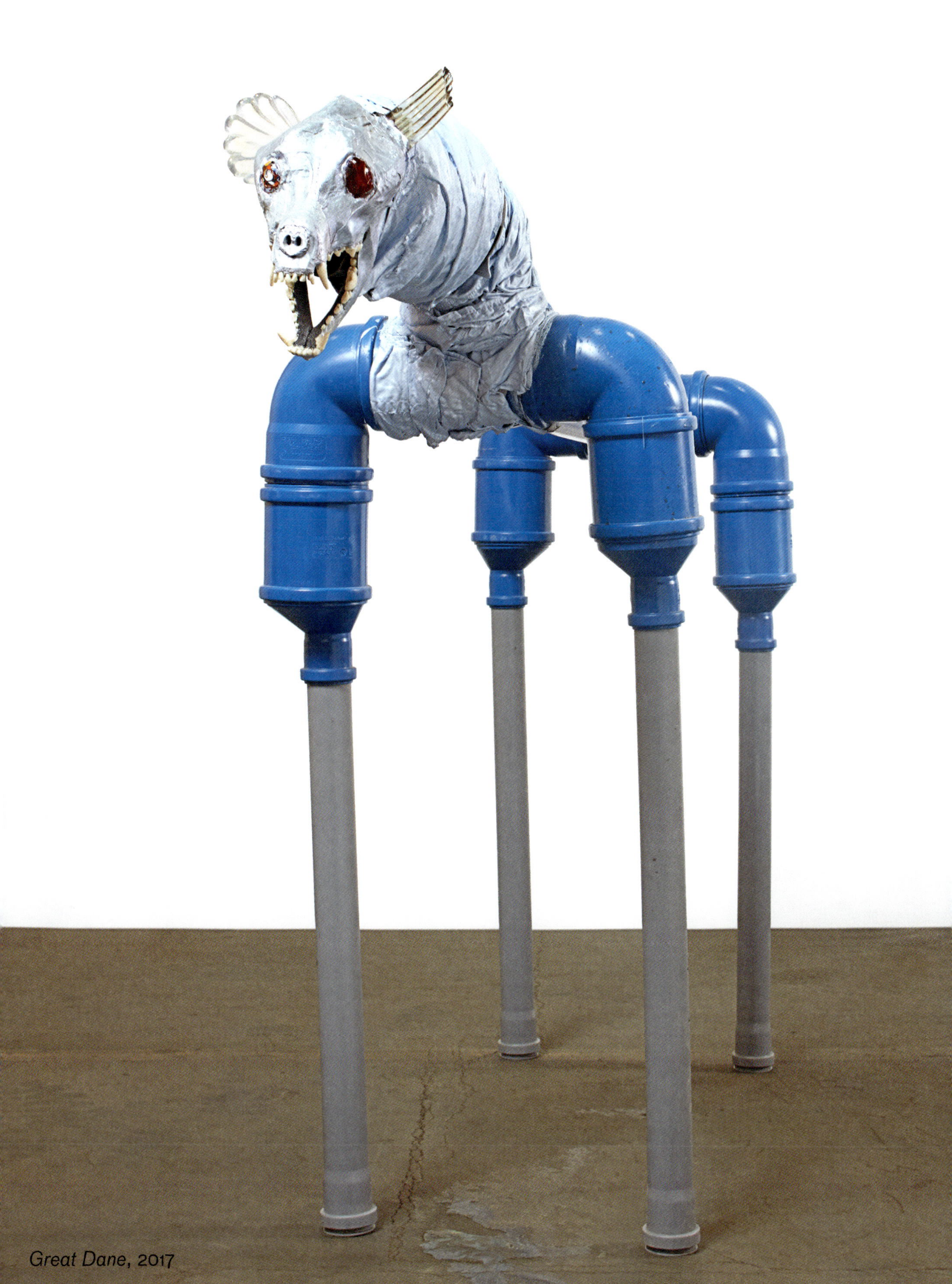

Great Dane, 2017

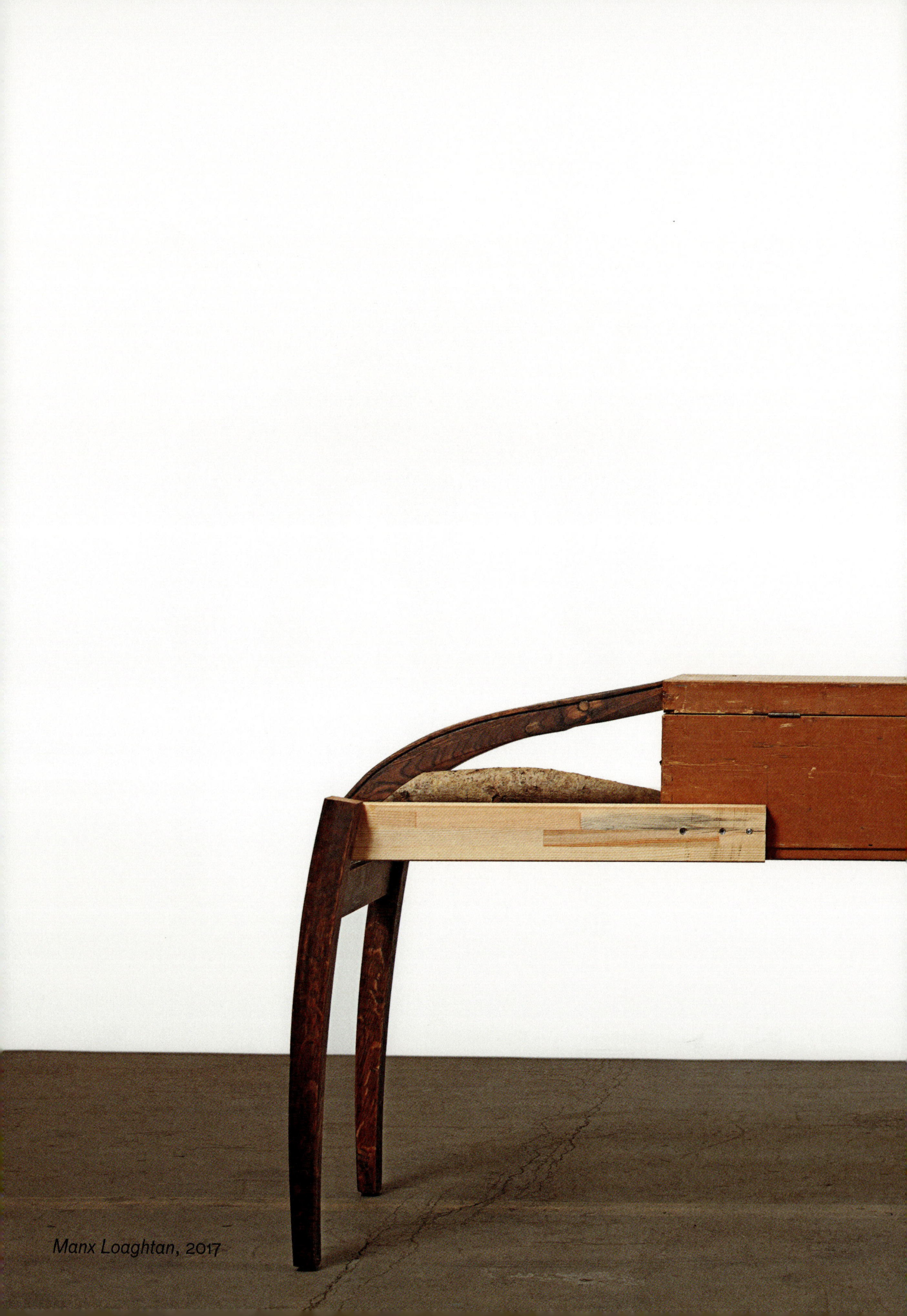

Manx Loaghtan, 2017

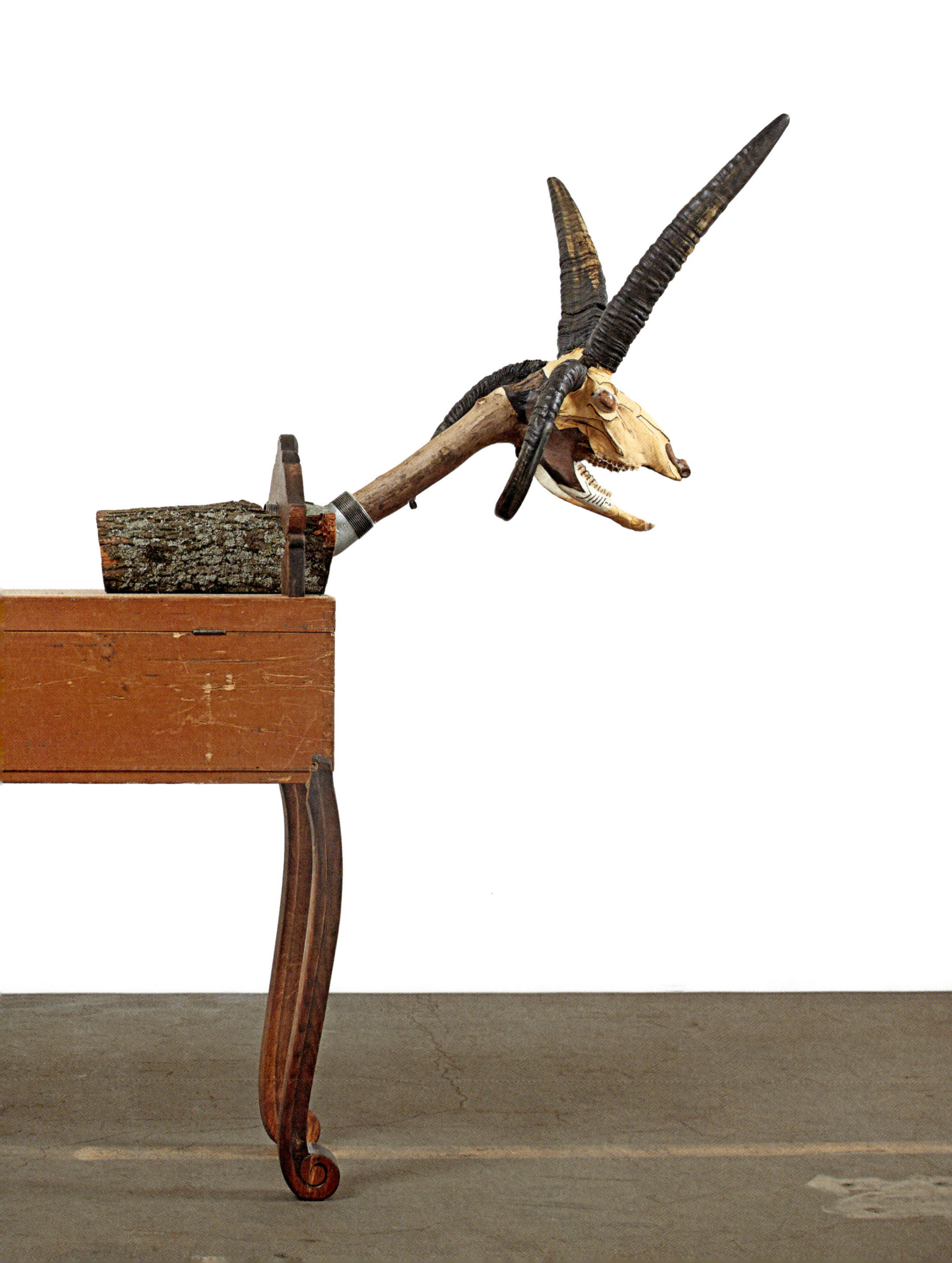

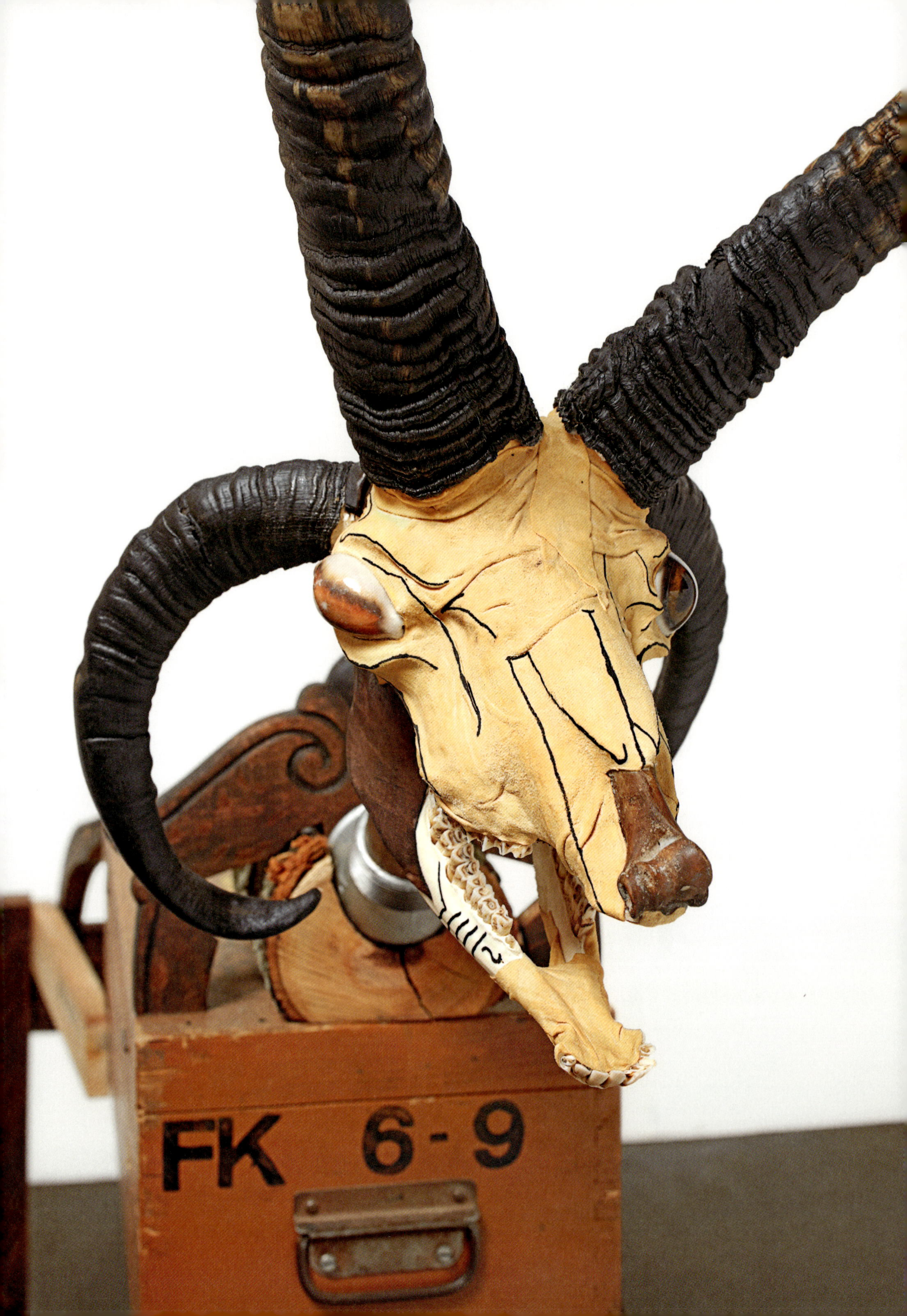
FK 6- 9

JIMMIE DURHAM'S GIFT TO EUROPE

HEIKE MUNDER

Jimmie Durham, who was born in the United States in 1940, is an artist, poet, writer, and former political activist. He launched his creative career in North America, complementing his political work for human rights and the rights of Indigenous people with a sculptural and performative practice that explored related issues: ethical questions and narratives informed by nationalist resentment. His sculptural assemblages harness his mostly white and educated audience's superficial ideas about nature and society. The artist tries to find visual analogies for these conceptions or stereotypical images, aiming to hold a mirror up to the beholder and nudge his or her concept of the Other toward a broader, more open perspective. After moving to Europe in 1994, Durham wrestled with his new geopolitical and cultural-historical environment: "I am looking always to engage some sort of European cultural history, like an interventionist place. Europe does like to be spiritual, it likes to imagine spirituality as the same as intellectuality."[1] He has a special relationship with Switzerland, and not just because he is interested in the cultural blend of an archaic belief in nature spirits and Calvinist gravity. In 1969, he enrolled at the École Supérieure des Beaux-Arts in Geneva, and it was then that he first worked with animal skulls, as a way to break with the lasting intellectual legacy of modernism. Skulls, he thought, were the perfect material for this endeavor.[2]

Animals have remained a constant in Durham's oeuvre. For the Migros Museum für Gegenwartskunst in Zurich, he has realized the project *God's Children, God's Poems* (2017). The artist turns the gallery into the scene of a congregation of fourteen sculptures. They are made out of the skulls of selected animal species studded with sometimes elaborate applications. Where ears or antlers were missing, he has mounted replicas; eyes cast out of colorful glass are set into the skulls. These modifications seem to breathe new life into the animals. The skulls Durham worked with represent a broad selection, ranging from the Manx Loaghtan, an almost mythical four-horned sheep native to the Isle of Man, to the ordinary European wild boar. The former has been given an understated paint job, whereas the latter is coated in "chamaleon"-type automotive paint and enhanced with pipes that protrude from the former nostrils like rifle barrels.

1   Johannes Schlebrügge, "Conversation with Jimmie Durham," *KünstlerInnenporträts* 53 (Vienna, 2000), www.mip.at/attachments/241 (accessed April 5, 2017).

2   Jean Fisher, "Jimmie Durham: Attending to Words and Bones. An Interview with Jean Fisher," *Art and Design*, no. 7–8 (1995), pp. 47–55.

For the wolf—its skull, too, has been sprayed with the iridescent car paint—Durham has built a metal body, with a neck made of pipes and a back fashioned out of industrial sheet metal. These mixed-media prostheses—besides metal, the artist has used wood, fabric, and other materials—match the real dimensions of the animals' bodies. At the same time, some of the sculptural assemblages have an air of mechanical contraptions, as though to exorcise nature from the creatures. The sculptures enliven the white and ostensibly neutral gallery, taking possession of it and, like lone animals, demarcating territories, stalking each other or crossing paths. The skulls come from different locations across Europe and represent a variety of species of wild as well as domesticated animals. From the four-horned sheep and the wild boar to the brown bear, the elk, the Tuscan Maremmana cattle, and the Great Dane: what they have in common is that each is the largest representative of its species.[3]

Durham casts these animals—or more properly speaking, animal skulls—as the protagonists of his own agenda. One question he broaches is that of the deconstruction of cultural-ethnic authenticity. The basis for such a deconstruction is the unmasking of cultural principles of classification and construction—in particular, the dualism of nature and culture. Durham's selection of animals undercuts this simplistic distinction, for example through the use of skulls of wild animals that owe their existence today to breeding efforts, like the bison/wisent, an endangered European species of bison. Others, including the brown bear and the Eurasian lynx, have been reintroduced to their erstwhile habitats. The concomitant disintegration of rigid classificatory schemes is now under discussion in various academic disciplines, including cultural animal studies, where thinkers not only seek to abandon the definition of the animal as a natural object but also critique the distinction between animal and human being founded on the definition of man as the subject of culture.[4]

A similar shift of perspective commenced in the arts in the 1960s, but it has remained a marginal phenomenon. Art movements such as performance or conceptual art have integrated animals into their spheres of activity, though largely as mute extras. One exception was Jannis Kounellis, who, in 1969, brought twelve live horses into the gallery in a radical effort not only to upset the established conception

---

3   See the "Register of Animals" in the present volume, compiled by Lea Altner.
4   See Roland Borgards, ed., *Tiere: Kulturwissenschaftliches Handbuch* (Stuttgart: Springer, 2016), p. 3.

of sculpture, but also to reenvision the art space as a social setting.[5] The animals took center stage in this work. Other artists including Ana Mendieta and Hermann Nitsch used animal blood, a substance they credited with a purifying magical or even universal power that also transcended the dividing line between human and animal. In the 1990s, artists questioned the authenticity of the animal as a natural object—see, for example, the sculptural work of Damian Hirst, who preserved cadavers in formaldehyde, or Mark Dion's conceptual use of specimens prepared for scientific purposes.[6]

Kounellis turned his horses into performers; Durham similarly stages his animal sculptures as social agents in the gallery space. By presenting these non-human beings as the equals of human "actants," he resorts to a conceptual framework that evinces parallels with the sociologist and philosopher Bruno Latour's actor-network theory, in which the classical dichotomies between subject and object, between culture and nature are suspended. This abstract intellectual theory can begin to dismantle cultural conventions. With its firm roots in the discourse of Western reason, its terminology makes it more accessible than other modes of thought such as animism. Animism, too, overrides the dichotomies between subject and object or culture and nature, according the potential for action and even agency properly speaking to non-human actants such as animals, plants, and things. For a long time, the reception of animism was bound up with modernity's colonialist faith in progress, a perspective in which animists appeared as primitives incapable of discriminating between animate and inanimate matter.[7] The belief in the ensoulment of object-worlds was rejected as incompatible with a rational logic. But as postmodern theory has looked to other systems of thought for guidance—a trend illustrated by developments such as cultural animal studies, posthumanism, and new materialism—the question of animism has been revisited as well.

Animism is now described as a relational mode of thinking that calls the central position of the human being, what is known as "Western anthropocentrism," into question. Durham's sculptures—consider the wolf, which is part animal, part machine—render inoperative the prevailing ontology on which the theory of the social rests, deliberately confusing the concepts of subject and object. In that sense, his practice

5   See Nike Bätzner, ed., *Arte Povera: Manifeste, Statements, Kritiken* (Basel: G+B Fine Arts, 1995), where Kounellis is quoted as saying that "the horses come from a social and political structure, they relate to a classical situation. They're directed against a mentality that's characteristic of Anglo-Saxons, the rational mentality [...] But in my case it became a social space, because the gallery owner didn't just sell, he provided a certain orientation. Putting the horses in that space served to engender a tension, to make a cut in the communication of art. In a situation like the one that prevailed in 1969, you made progress not gradually but through radical tensions." Ibid., pp. 150–151.

6   See also Jessica Ullrich, "Tiere und Bildende Kunst," in Borgards, *Tiere*, pp. 201–202.

7   See the definition of "animism" proposed by Edward B. Tylor, *Primitive Culture* (1871), quoted in Irene Albers and Anselm Franke, eds., *Nach dem Animismus* (Berlin: Kadmos, 2016), p. 9.

may be read as a variant of animism: it is invested in the power of
transformation, in blurred boundaries and the possibility that entails
of keeping a narrative open. Durham noted in conversation that his
exhibition project for the Migros Museum für Gegenwartskunst is meant
to give animals their souls back. The British writer Jean Fisher has
written that Durham introduces us to a cosmology in which the world
is not regarded, evaluated, and colonized through the narrow lens
of an object status that ensures the predominance of human actants.
Instead, it is seen as an integral whole in which all elements—
animate as well as inanimate ones—are partners interconnected by
symmetrical relationships.[8]

Since the beginning of Durham's career as an artist, dismantling the
linearity of time—from life to death—has been a crucial theme in his
work and thinking. In an interview, Durham said: "For more than thirty
years I have seen every dead bird and animal every day wherever I am.
So it became necessary to see if that was a usable gift or just a dirty
trick that would drive me crazy."[9] He turns this sensitivity to death—
whose presence tends to be camouflaged in Western contexts due to
a deep-seated cultural bias—into a method: he brings the animals
back into the present by giving them new bodies, altering the skulls to
individualize them and thus endowing the sculptures with a soul in
the animistic sense. In so doing, Durham relies on a "trick" that, as
the anthropologist Michael Taussig has shown, serves to lend the
appearance of the magical to events or stories.[10] This magic acts as
a projection screen for the human yearning for an all-encompassing
worldview integrating spiritual elements that have no home in Western
reason. With his animals for *God's Children, God's Poems*, Durham
takes up this yearning, charting a course between satisfying the desire
for spirituality and opening it up to more complex contexts and per-
spectives. His project is not meant to reactivate a Romantic notion of
union with nature; rather, it is a gift that prompts us to reflect on the
rich diversity of nature and the subject's multiple roles in it. We might
also say: Durham teaches us to be tolerant of ambiguity, challenging
us o abandon a thinking in rigid categories, to acknowledge and appre-
ciate plural meanings and contradictions, and to question engrained
modes of thinking and manifest constellations of power.[11]

8   See also Jean Fisher, "Foreword: Stranger at the Gate," in Jimmie Durham, *Waiting to Be Interrupted* (Milan and
    Antwerp: Mousse, 2014), p. viii.

9   Lucy Lippard, "Jimmie Durham: Postmodernist Savage," *Art in America*, February 1993, p. 65.

10   Michael Taussig, "The Stories Things Tell and Why They Tell Them," *e-flux*, no. 36 (July 2012),
    http://www.e-flux.com/journal/36/61256/the-stories-things-tell-and-why-they-tell-them/ (accessed April 18, 2017).

11   Verena Krieger, "Ambiguitätstoleranz als pädagogisches Ziel," in Verena Krieger and Rachel Mader, eds.,
    Ambiguität in der Kunst: Typen und Funktionen eines ästhetischen Paradigmas (Vienna: Böhlau, 2010), pp. 16–17.

*JIMMIE DURHAMS GESCHENK
AN EUROPA*

HEIKE MUNDER

Jimmie Durham, geboren 1940 in den USA, ist Künstler, Poet, Autor, ehemals politischer Aktivist und begann seine künstlerische Karriere in den USA. Parallel zu seiner politischen Arbeit für Menschenrechte und für die Rechte indigener Völker entwickelte er eine skulpturale und performative Praxis, in der er sich ebenfalls mit ethischen Fragen und nationalistisch geprägten Narrativen auseinandersetzte. In seinen skulpturalen Assemblagen macht er sich dafür die vermeintlichen Vorstellungen über Natur und Gesellschaft seines meist weissen und gut gebildeten Publikums zunutze. Durham versucht, diesen Auffassungen oder auch klischierten Bildern visuell zu entsprechen mit dem Ziel, dem Betrachter den Spiegel entgegenzuhalten und das Denken des Anderen für eine breitere Perspektive zu öffnen. Seit 1994 lebt Durham in Europa und reibt sich seitdem an seiner neuen geopolitischen und kulturgeschichtlichen Umgebung: «I am looking always to engage some sort of European cultural history, like an interventionist place. Europe does like to be spiritual, it likes to imagine spirituality as the same as intellectuality.»[1] Zur Schweiz hat er einen besonderen Bezug – nicht nur, weil ihn die kulturelle Mischung von archaischem Glauben an Naturgeister und calvinistischem Ernst interessiert. 1969 kam er zum Studium an die Genfer Kunsthochschule École Supérieure des Beaux-Arts. In dieser Zeit verwendete er zum ersten Mal Tierschädel als Arbeitsmaterial. Für diese Entscheidung grundlegend war der Wunsch, mit den anhaltenden modernistischen Vorstellungen zu brechen. Die Schädel erschienen ihm damals als das perfekte Ausgangsmaterial dafür.[2]

Tiere blieben eine Konstante in Durhams Schaffen. Für das Migros Museum für Gegenwartskunst in Zürich realisierte er das Projekt *God's Children, God's Poems* (2017). Der Künstler versammelt 14 Skulpturen im Ausstellungsraum. Diese sind aus Schädeln ausgewählter Tierarten gefertigt, an die er teils aufwendige Applikationen anbrachte – falls Ohren oder Geweihe fehlten, diese neu montierte und die Schädel mit Augen aus buntem gegossenem Glas versetzte. Durch diese Modifikationen erscheinen die Tiere erneut zum Leben erweckt. Die bearbeiteten Schädel repräsentieren eine breite Auswahl, die vom beinahe mythischen Vierhornschaf, dem Manx Loaghtan von der Isle of Man, bis zum ordinären europäischen Wildschwein reicht. Ersteres bemalte Durham dezent – Letzteres wurde mit dem Autolack «Chamäleon» lackiert und mit Rohren versehen, die wie Gewehrkolben aus den ehemaligen Nasenlöchern starren. Dem Wolf, dessen Schädel ebenso mit dem gleichen irisierenden Autolack besprüht wurde, wurde ein Körper aus Metall gebaut, dessen Hals aus Rohren und dessen Rücken aus Industrieblech gefertigt ist. Die Körper aus Assemblagen verschiedener Materialien – etwa Holz, Metall und Textilien – entsprechen den realen Dimensionen von Tieren. Gleichzeitig schwingt bei so mancher dieser skulpturalen Assemblagen ein maschinenhaftes Moment mit: Die Natur wird diesen Kreaturen geradezu abspenstig gemacht. Die Skulpturen beleben den weissen, angeblich neutralen Ausstellungsraum. Sie bemächtigen sich seiner und stecken wie Einzelgänger ihr Territorium ab, beleben es oder durchkreuzen es gar. Die verwendeten Schädel stammen aus unterschiedlichen Gebieten Europas und repräsentieren die Vertreter unterschiedlicher Spezies sowohl von Wild- als auch von Zuchttieren. Vom sogenannten Vierhornschaf über das Wildschwein, den Braunbären und den Elch zum toskanischen Maremmaner Rind bis hin zur Deutschen Dogge: Gemeinsam ist ihnen, dass sie die jeweils grössten Tiere ihrer biologischen Art sind.[3]

1   Johannes Schlebrügge, «Conversation with Jimmie Durham», in: *KünstlerInnenporträts* 53 (Wien 2000), www.mip.at/attachments/241 (abgerufen am 5.4.2017).

2   Jean Fisher, «Jimmie Durham. Attending to Words and Bones. An Interview with Jean Fisher», in: *Art and Design*, Bd. 10, Nr. 7–8 (1995), S. 47–55.

3   Siehe «Tierregister» in diesem Katalog, zusammengestellt von Lea Altner.

Durham macht diese Tiere oder besser Tierschädel zu Akteuren seiner eigenen Agenda. Eine Frage, die er damit aufgreift, ist jene nach der Dekonstruktion von kulturell-ethnischer Authentizität. Grundlage für diese Dekonstruktion ist die Entlarvung von kulturellen Klassifizierungs- und Konstruktionsprinzipien – insbesondere des Dualismus von Natur und Kultur. Durhams Tierauswahl unterläuft diese vereinfachte Unterscheidung – beispielsweise indem er Schädel von Wildtieren benutzt, die aus einer Zucht stammen: etwa von Wisenten, einer vom Aussterben bedrohten europäischen Bison-Art. Ebenso sind es Tiere aus Wiederansiedlungen – wie der Braunbär oder der eurasische Luchs. Die damit einhergehende Auflösung von rigiden Klassifikationen wird inzwischen in verschiedenen Fachrichtungen diskutiert, so den Cultural Animal Studies. Diese versuchen, nicht nur die Definition des Tiers als Naturobjekt aufzugeben, sondern üben auch Kritik an der Tier-Mensch-Unterscheidung, die sich auf die Definition des Menschen als Kultursubjekt stützt.[4]

Auch in der Kunst gibt es seit den 1960er Jahren diesen Perspektivwechsel – allerdings nur als Randerscheinung. Kunstrichtungen wie die Performance-Kunst oder Konzeptkunst integrieren Tiere in ihre Handlungsfelder, wenn auch eher als Statisten. Eine Ausnahme bildet dabei Jannis Kounellis, der 1969 zwölf lebende Pferde in den Ausstellungsraum brachte, um damit nicht nur den Skulpturenbegriff auf den Kopf zu stellen, sondern auch den Ausstellungsraum zum sozialen Raum zu erklären.[5] Kounellis räumte den Tieren in dieser Arbeit die Hauptrolle ein. Künstlerinnen und Künstler wie etwa Ana Mendieta und Hermann Nitsch verwendeten Tierblut. Sie schreiben diesem eine reinigende, magische oder auch universelle Macht zu, die zugleich die Grenze zwischen Mensch und Tier aufhebt. In den 1990er Jahren befragten Künstler die Authentizität des Tiers als Naturobjekt – so etwa die skulpturalen Arbeiten Damian Hirsts, der Tiere in Formaldehyd einlegte, oder Mark Dions konzeptuelle Verwendung von naturwissenschaftlich präparierten Tieren.[6]

So wie Kounellis seine Pferde zu Performern machte, erhebt Durham seine tierischen Skulpturen zu sozialen Akteuren im Ausstellungsraum. Indem er diese nicht menschlichen Lebewesen mit den Menschen auf eine Ebene von «Aktanten» stellt, greift er ein Denkschema auf, das Parallelen mit der Akteur-Netzwerk-Theorie des Soziologen und Philosophen Bruno Latour aufweist. Mit diesem werden die klassischen Dichotomien zwischen Subjekt und Objekt, zwischen Kultur und Natur aufgehoben. Diese abstrakte Gedankenkonstruktion vermag es, kulturelle Konventionen aufzuweichen. Ihre fest im westlich-rationalen Diskurs verankerte Terminologie vereinfacht scheinbar die Rezeption dieser Theorie im Vergleich zu anderen Denkformen wie dem Animismus. Der Animismus hebt die Dichotomien zwischen Subjekt und Objekt oder Kultur und Natur auf und gesteht nicht menschlichen Aktanten wie Tieren, Pflanzen und Dingen Handlungspotenzial oder sogar Handlungsmacht zu. Die Rezeption des Animismus war lange Zeit mit der kolonialen, fortschrittsgläubigen Haltung der Moderne verknüpft. Aus dieser Perspektive wurden Animisten als Primitive wahrgenommen, die nicht in der Lage waren, zwischen belebter und unbelebter Materie zu unterscheiden.[7] Damals wurde der Glaube an die Beseelung von Objektwelten aus einer rationalen Logik heraus abgelehnt. Doch in dem Masse, wie die postmoderne Theorie sich an anderen

4　Siehe Roland Borgards (Hg.), *Tiere. Kulturwissenschaftliches Handbuch*, Stuttgart 2016, S. 3.

5　Jannis Kounellis in: Nike Bätzner (Hg.), *Arte Povera – Manifeste, Statements, Kritiken*, Basel 1995, S. 150 f.: «Die Pferde kommen aus einer gesellschaftlichen und politischen Struktur, sie nehmen auf eine klassische Situation Bezug. Sie wenden sich gegen eine Mentalität, die charakteristisch für Angelsachsen ist, nämlich rational ... Aber in meinem Fall wurde sie zum gesellschaftlichen Raum, weil der Galerist nicht nur verkaufte, sondern eine bestimmte Orientierung gab. Die Pferde in jenen Raum zu stellen, diente dazu, eine Spannung zu erzeugen, einen Schnitt in der Kommunikation der Kunst. In einer Situation wie 1969 ging man nicht stufenweise voran, sondern über radikale Spannungen.»

6　Siehe auch Jessica Ullrich, «Tiere und Bildende Kunst», in: Borgards, *Tiere* (Anm. 4), S. 201 f.

7　Definition «Animismus» nach Edward B. Tylor, *Primitive Culture* (1871), in: Irene Albers, Anselm Franke (Hg.), *Nach dem Animismus*, Berlin 2016, S. 9.

Denkschemata orientierte – wie am Beispiel der Cultural Animal Studies, des Post-Humanism oder des New Materialism zu erkennen ist –, wurde auch das Verständnis des Animismus einer Revision unterzogen.

Heute wird der Animismus als relationale Denkweise verstanden, welche die Position des Menschen im Zentrum, den «westlichen Anthropozentrismus», infrage stellt. Durham setzt mit seinen Skulpturen – wie im Beispiel des Wolfs, der teils Tier, teils Maschine ist – die vorherrschende sozialtheoretische Ontologie ausser Kraft und betreibt ein Verwirrspiel zwischen Subjekt und Objekt. Seine Praxis könnte als eine Spielart des Animismus gelesen werden: das Setzen auf die Kraft der Verwandlung, auf unklare Grenzen und damit auch auf die Möglichkeit, eine Erzählung offenzuhalten. Im Gespräch sagte Durham, dass er mit dem Ausstellungsprojekt für das Migros Museum für Gegenwartskunst den Tieren ihre Seele zurückgeben möchte. Die britische Autorin Jean Fisher konstatierte, dass wir es bei Durham mit einer Kosmologie zu tun haben, in der die Welt nicht in jenem Objektstatus betrachtet, bewertet oder kolonialisiert wird, in dem menschliche Aktanten die Oberhand innehaben. Stattdessen wird sie als ungeteiltes Ganzes wahrgenommen, in dem alle Elemente – lebende wie nicht lebende – in symmetrischer Weise in einer partnerschaftlichen Beziehung stehen.[8]

Seit Beginn seiner künstlerischen Karriere nimmt die Auflösung der linearen Zeitfolge – vom Leben zum Tod – eine wesentliche Rolle im Arbeiten und Denken Durhams ein. In einem Interview sagte Durham: «For more than thirty years I have seen every dead bird and animal every day wherever I am. So it became necessary to see if that was a usable gift or just a dirty trick that would drive me crazy.»[9] Diese Sensibilität dem Toten gegenüber – etwas, das, kulturell bedingt, häufig in westlichen Kontexten ausgeblendet wird – macht er zu seiner Methode: Er holt das Tier wieder in die Gegenwart, indem er ihm einen neuen Körper verleiht, die Schädel durch seine Bearbeitungen zu Individuen erhebt und der Skulptur damit eine Seele im animistischen Sinne zuspricht. Durham benutzt damit einen «Trick», den auch der Anthropologe Michael Taussig beschreibt, um Geschehnisse beziehungsweise Geschichten magisch erscheinen zu lassen.[10] Diese Magie dient als Projektionsfläche für die menschliche Sehnsucht nach einem allumfassenden Weltbild, nach der Integration spiritueller Elemente, die in einem westlich rationalen Kontext nicht selbstverständlich sind. Mit seinen Tieren für *God's Children, God's Poems* macht Durham sich diese Sehnsucht zu eigen und bewegt sich zwischen der Befriedigung dieses Begehrens und dessen Öffnung hin zu komplexeren Zusammenhängen und Perspektiven. Dieses Projekt soll keine Reaktivierung eines romantischen Bildes über das Einssein mit der Natur sein, sondern ein Geschenk, dass zur Reflexion über die Vielfalt von Natur und die Rolle des Subjekts darin anregt. Man könnte auch sagen: Durham lehrt den Betrachter Ambiguitätstoleranz – das heisst: nicht in rigiden Kategorien zu denken, sondern Vieldeutigkeiten und Widersprüche wahrzunehmen und zuzulassen und damit eingefahrene Denkweisen und manifestierte Machtkonstellationen zu hinterfragen.[11]

8   Siehe auch Jean Fisher, «Foreword: Stranger at the Gate», in: Jimmie Durham, *Waiting to Be Interrupted*, Mailand, Antwerpen 2014, S. VIII.

9   Lucy Lippard, «Jimmie Durham: Postmodernist Savage», in: *Art in America* (Februar 1993), S. 65.

10   Michael Taussig, «Was Dinge erzählen und warum sie es tun», in: Albers, Franke, *Nach dem Animismus* (Anm. 7), S. 190.

11   Verena Krieger, «Ambiguitätstoleranz als pädagogisches Ziel», in: Verena Krieger, Rachel Mader (Hg.), *Ambiguität in der Kunst. Typen und Funktionen eines ästhetischen Paradigmas*, Wien 2010, S. 16 f.

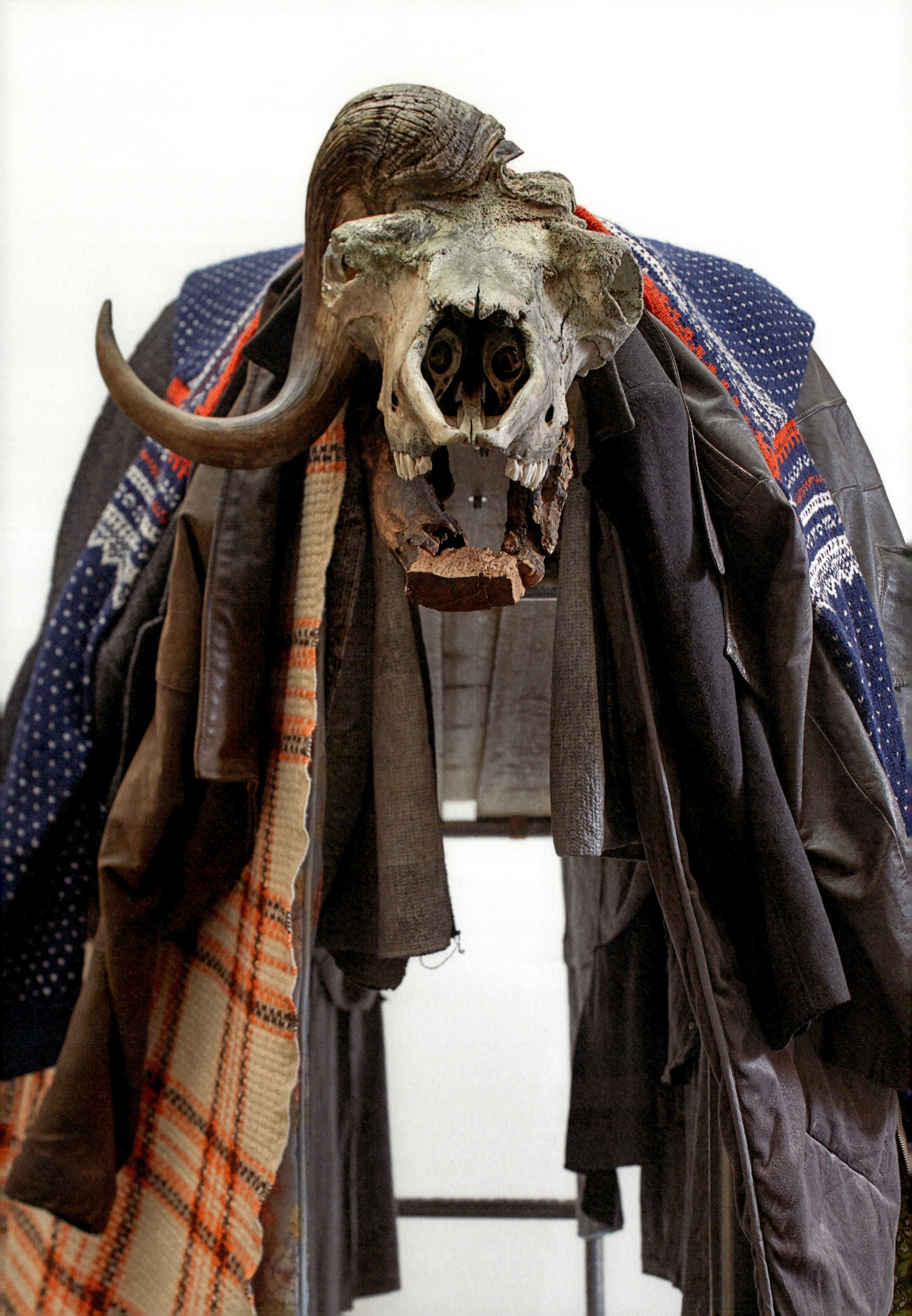

NINE DAYS LIVING AMONGST THE VERY LARGE ANIMALS OF EUROPE

RICHARD WILLIAM HILL

… after that, Durham begins to work again on the skull of the brown bear. It has already been partially covered in pieces of a tan-colored chamois and both of its eyes are in place. The right eye is an orb of tan-colored glass with streaks in it, the most notable being a curving line of black that swells in width, turns ninety degrees and then thins out and tapers off. The glass is colored but opaque, so that it shines, but lacks depth. Still, the movement provided by that black line gives a sense of fierce, almost manic energy. The left eye is made from a very dark-brown and black, slightly misshapen piece of glass, also nearly opaque. The odd shape of the glass—it is a Murano glassmaker's discard—gives the impression of a slightly bulging, forward-facing pupil. An arcing line of light-blue paint intensifies the sense of forward orientation. Durham tells me later that he does not want the eyes of his animals to be fully lifelike: "I do want to show the death of these animals, I don't want to pretend that they are alive [...] but that death is not *so* permanent as we might think." He also tells me that in choosing the material he is, "trying to see what object would make that dead animal see better in his death. He wouldn't see like living things see, so the eye has to be very special, but it doesn't mean it has to look like a real eye."

I will learn in a few minutes that the chamois is attached by soaking it in a watered-down solution of glue for a number of hours and then applying additional glue to both contact surfaces while it is still wet. This allows it to be stretched, skin-like, over the bony skull. Chamois leather is traditionally from European Chamois goats, although the commercial product is now more likely to be from domestic goats and sheep. I learn about the application method by watching Durham do the same thing now with pieces of brown leather that he has begun to apply across the back of the skull. Later he will add strips of ornate wood molding, to "make it look very European," and then some color-ful glass shards and tiles that change its character again, making it more colorfully ornate and somehow less fierce. Its body will be a mus-cularly twisting length of olive wood.

I started this essay mid-sentence because that best reflects my own encounter with these works. My writing deadline, for good practical reasons having to do with editing, translation, and catalogue produc-tion, means that there will be no opportunity to see the completed works I have committed to writing about. I have nevertheless made sure to visit Durham's studio while the work is in progress, awkwardly nudging a nine-day trip from Vancouver to Berlin into my schedule in mid-March. In Berlin, I spent almost all my time with Durham, visiting the studio, photographing and shooting video, chatting and mostly just watching the work being done and the objects emerging. Two of Durham's assistants were present much of the time: Kai Vollmer, who has been with Durham for a number of years helping with the administrative side of many things and with the fabrication of objects, and William Nicholson, who works part-time in the studio helping with fabrication. He works primarily on the body of a bear while I am there. Occasionally, I helped out myself, moving things around or cutting wood as seemed helpful. Nothing was entirely completed by the time I left, but I had a headful of images and ideas to digest. Let me begin formally with some setting of cultural context.

The Anthropological Context
The reader is likely aware of a group of people known for their fascination with, and deep connection to, animals. You may argue that all human beings are intrigued by animals in one way or another and this is true. But the people I want to discuss have, if I can be permitted to generalize, a distinctive, culture-wide affinity for animals. They decorate their clothing, dwellings, and important community sites with animal imagery, often using this imagery totemically, to indicate their membership in particular social groups or warrior societies. They sometimes name themselves after animals: "Wolf," "Eagle," "Raven," or "Bear," for example, to associate themselves with the powers and attributes they believe these animals have. More importantly, many—perhaps the most spiritually developed—have established close personal relationships with them, treating them with sympathy as fellow beings. Of course, their understanding of their animal kin is rarely scientific and at times distorts the true character of particular animals to meet mythic societal imperatives. Still, this cultural context must be understood to make sense of Durham's project. I am speaking, of course, about Europeans.

Joking aside, I want to emphasize the extent to which Durham's project is an attempt to participate in an ongoing European conversation about animals. It is an intervention in that conversation, just as any intellectually valuable perspective would be, but it is not a view from outside. Durham has lived in Europe for decades and grew up in a nation-state created by European settlers. The questions his artworks pose in this exhibition are his participation in a global conversation about how we might better understand the relationship between ourselves and animals. It is, therefore, about the many dichotomies the European tradition has created to categorize and define our relationship to the non-human world. Most recently these discussions have centered around new materialism, object oriented ontology, non-humanization, and the recent declaration of the Anthropocene. We are starting to see, perhaps, that these systems of difference between nature and culture, animal and human, domestic and wild animals conceal an incredible traffic and mutual dependence both materially and conceptually.

The focus on the size of the animals is part of the European dimension of the project. Some have simply evolved to be large, like the giant musk ox or elk. Even the famously huge Maremmana cattle, which look as though they have walked out of a European cave painting, seem simply to have started their relationship with humans as very large animals. Others, like the Great Dane are, as Durham tells me, "made by humans to be as big as they could make them. All other people have dogs and they never thought to make great giant ones, it's a special, European idea." But, he adds, "the dogs are always nice animals," and usually easy to befriend.

By attending to their scale, Durham draws attention to how we value animals. He said, "I think hamsters and shrews and moles and many kinds of mice are extraordinary, special animals, but humans in general think great big animals are the most impressive and important animals. [...] In reality, we're all brothers and sisters."

Skulls

I am hesitant to begin with the skulls, because they are so easily misunderstood, but there is no choice. If it is the most challenging aspect of the work, it is also the start of each work and the object out of which each sculpture's body will take shape. This was very clear in the studio. When I arrived, most of the skulls had already been materially elaborated upon in one way or another by the artist, but none yet had bodies. The Ibex skull had been given large taxidermy eyes intended for a moose, which bulge in its sockets. The skull itself is painted green. It also has a "neck" comprised of, from back to front: a length of metal pipe, an elaborately carved section of old ornamental wood molding that the artist acquired in Turin, and a relatively new lathed section of a chair or table leg. It merely waits for a body. These will be more chair parts, because Durham sees a connection between the elegant curve of the antler and the graceful curves of chair parts.

Some skulls are still bare and, like the musk ox, may remain so. Later in the week, on Friday, the skull of a Maremmana bull arrives, crated like a work of art. I open the crate and lift the skull out onto a blanket on the floor. Durham sits by it and studies it carefully.

Unlike most of the other skulls, it is weathered by time and probably also exposure to the elements. There is a neat round hole in the top of the skull, over the brain cavity (although just barely), no doubt the fatal wound from the slaughter house. When I asked him what happens when a skull arrives and he begins to consider it, he tells me, "I don't know what that is, but I know it's not dissimilar to when I meet a fellow being that's alive, a human, a gorilla, a cow, a dog—you look at each other in the face right away. Most animals don't like to be stared at. If you want to be friends, you look at them, blink, turn away, and then they trust you." Staring is an "attack mode," but all the same "we still look at each other in the face" to make sense of each other. It is not a simple "looking at," like voyeurs at the zoo, but instead an attempt to carefully read and decode them, as we do human faces, "to see them, each individually."

Durham tells me that each work, starting from the skull, is his effort to express and honor the spirit of the particular animal. This is a dangerous phrase, easily understood to mean many different things. I know from long experience that the most treacherous for Durham is an association with some notion of Indigenous mysticism. I want to use (and then quickly discard) my authority as a writer of Indigenous heritage (in my case, mostly Cree) to assure you that while Durham no doubt has drawn on his Cherokee intellectual heritage one way and another throughout his life, he is in no way reflecting a "Cherokee perspective" in this work. There is not a trove of hidden mystical Cherokee wisdom, always just out of reach that, if you but knew it, would explain everything. Durham is a profoundly original thinker who has engaged critically and innovatively with many, many different cultural situations and intellectual traditions, including those of his Indigenous heritage. He is not typical in any way, which is what makes him so interesting.

During my visit I never asked him to define the term spirit. Not being very spiritual myself, I take it to mean a kind of summation of that animal's character, appearance, life force, energy, and so forth, in a way that, in concert, is powerful and important, but ineffable; something that must be approached, in large part, poetically. As he put it to me, "I want to decorate all these skulls as though I were a European decorating skulls, so I've tried to use European things, like glass, cloth, paint." The task, however, is to "bring back the spirit of this animal and not the representation of this animal" in a mimetic sense. This depends on his audience being willing to extend themselves: "One doesn't ever succeed in artwork [...] one succeeds at some level and real success is the cooperation between the work, the artist, and the public. So we'll see." The work in this exhibition is therefore part of a conversation with his fellow humans—or perhaps part of a conversation out of which we might work out together what it is to be humans-in-the-world, rather than humans trying to transcend the world, or hold dominion over it. If, as the work suggests, we are deeply implicated in the lives of animals and they are not radically other to us, then we must also not be what we thought we were either.

For Durham, working with the skulls itself helps to clarify the moral dimension of our relationship to animals. "When I work with the skulls, I see very clearly how we really are all of the same family, I see that their skulls are *like* our skulls, their bodies are *like* our bodies." This kinship has a particular character for us, because "every animal responds to human love. It sounds corny to say that, but every animal will. Every animal is kind of waiting for love and friendship, every animal is waiting for a momentary lack of danger and lack of hunger. I've known it since I was a child. And it's something great and strange at the same time to be a human, therefore. It means a privilege, it means a responsibility."

When I arrive, the enormous Shire Horse skull has already been given the foundation of a neck in the form of a heavy wooden plank, supplemented by sections of unmilled wood. It has ears made of wood and a thin, bright, and shiny sheet of copper that has been crumpled up and placed into the nose cavity, where it suggests to me the horse's steaming breath, a sign, perhaps, of its life force. If you have ever been around horses, you will have noticed the force of their breath. Almost all of these aspects will be changed before I leave. But what strikes me at the moment is how incredibly fierce the horse looks; malevolent even. The suggestion of ferocity comes from the shape of the eye socket itself and the way in which the ridge above the eye arches up in what I want to interpret as a gleefully malicious scowl. Likewise, the upward curving line of his jaw suggests a matching sinister grin. This is a trait they share with human skulls, which are often said to grin (presumably it is the grinning skull that makes the Jolly Roger jolly). But looking around at the skulls made it clear that the fiercely arched eye ridge is particular to the large herbivores. The bear, lynx, and Great Dane look fierce because of their gaping mouths and dangerous fangs, but the fierce appearance of the herbivores is just an accident of evolution, informative of the anatomy of the animal, but not a semiotic facial expression, nor a directly expressive indication of its character. Covered with muscle and skin, all of these animals are capable of using their faces expressively in ways that humans can at least partially decode. But the artist must contend with the fact that the bare bone is also accidentally expressive, often powerfully so. In cases such as the Manx Loaghtan four-horned sheep,

a breed from the Isle of Man, Durham allows that expressiveness to
show through.

The horse, however, will have his skull covered in ways that, like his
original flesh, come in around the eyes and jaw to conceal the fierce
skull beneath. This is a fascinating process to watch. When I arrive,
Durham has already taken fragments of a carved, curving railing and
has been attaching them to the neck and across the skull, in the
troughs of the jaw that are there to hold muscle. The railing is incredibly sinuous and makes me think about the way in which the things
we ake reflect our bodies and also how our bodies reflect other structures in the world. When I ask Durham about this later, he tells me
that he saw the sinuousness of the railing and was not surprised when
sections of it, fit perfectly, on the jaw. Yet not long afterward I watched
in surprise as he began covering many of these pieces with leather.
He told me that he had realized that his audience would see it too
distinctly, "as a piece of wood stuck onto the jaw bone" and therefore lose the sense of horse muscle. He did not want that to happen,
"so I covered it minimally with leather." This was not an attempt at
verisimilitude, which Durham is deeply suspicious of, but to capture
the animal's character through the materials. This requires not that
materials give the illusion that they are something they are not—he
has a horror of taxidermy and all forms of representational "realism"—
but the integration of the materials into the particular sculptural project.

Body Parts

As I have said, the bodies emerge, to a great extent, out of reflection
upon the skulls. But here it is worth pausing for a moment to consider
the intersectional character of these bodies and indeed the skulls
as well. Like so many of Durham's sculptures, their sources are diverse
and legion. An inventory would be misleading. You might say that
every animal sculpture here, one way or another, contains some or all
of the following: a lifetime's worth of walking around and exploring
various environments in many parts of the world, urban and rural; a lifetime's worth of socializing with human and non-human animals; a
lifetime's worth of talking with other people; a lifetime's worth of reading the words of authors and writing words of his own in poetry
and prose; a lifetime's worth of exploring, handling, and collecting
objects; a lifetime's worth of choosing, manipulating, adjusting,
painting, marking, carving, attaching, and otherwise changing and
re-arranging objects. This latter, his practice as a sculptor, is very
much the sum of all the others, or to put it another way, the practice
of managing the intersection of all these mental-material things is
a way of thinking socially, through materials, about ourselves and our

world. I have come to believe that the social dimension is as real a component of his practice as the bits of wood, metal, and so forth. Throughout my visit, Durham is constantly in conversations: in the studio, at the dinner table, during the wine after dinner.

The Berlin Animal Body-Part Stores
"In the next few days," Durham tells me, "I will need to visit the various animal body-parts stores of Berlin." When I look puzzled, he adds, deadpan (but clearly pleased to have a straight-man), "I am talking, of course, about used clothing stores, scrapyards, flea markets ..." Indeed, as soon as I arrive I can see that Durham is eager to get building the animals' bodies and anxious to get the necessary "art supplies." He has some items—he always does—that he may have carried with him for many years. In this case, glass rejects from the glass studios of Murano, sections of olive trees from the Apulia region of Italy, old moldings from Turin, bits of pipe and furniture parts from who knows where. But he needs much more.

On Monday afternoon, Vollmer drives us to the Humana Second-Hand-Kaufhaus, near Frankfurter Tor. It advertises itself on a front window as a "First Class Second-Hand-Markt." Here Durham is looking for heavy coats and blankets that would make a suitable body for the musk ox. The shop is large, with many floors, and it takes time to make our way through all the relevant sections, piling up so many coats, pants, and blankets that we overwhelm the cashier and she has to call in a colleague to handle the back-up of other customers unlucky enough to be stuck behind us. It cannot be helped. Musk oxen are big.

As I have already mentioned, Durham has decided to leave the musk ox skull as it is, except that he has replaced the missing bottom jaw with a piece of jaw-shaped unfinished wood. The skull is also missing a horn, and according to the person who provided it, this was because it had been fatally injured attacking a train. Listening to Durham discuss its body, which will be a pile of coats and blankets, I lack the imagination to see how effective this will actually be. A few days ago, Vollmer sent me a photograph of the completed work, which is astonishingly musk ox-like, while not for a moment deceiving you about the fact that it is a metal scaffolding draped with blankets and coats. Across the top is what looks to be a Sami-inspired sweater of the type you might get in Norway.

The next day I am extremely—it turns out naïvely—excited to be able to come on the trip to the scrap metal yard. Thanks to Hollywood I imagine us wandering amongst dismembered automobiles, shattered large appliances and other fascinating detritus, with Durham picking and choosing the items that he needs, especially items for the boar's body. When we arrive I make the mistake of filming Durham, which, it urns out, is strictly forbidden. Vollmer makes apologies in German, but by this point they have decided that they can't allow us to enter the area, due, they say, to the potential liability. Eventually they suggest another place not too far away that we might try, not far from the Schöneberg S-Bahn station. Arriving there I leave the camera in the car and we all head into the front office. There Vollmer learns that, again for liability reasons, only he can enter the yard and look for things. Durham and I must wait by the front gate for him to find things and bring them over to show us. He must also wear a fluorescent safety vest and sign a waiver that, as far as I can tell, exempts the propri- etors from blame should they happen to accidentally kill or maim him during his visit. And, once again, this time unprovoked or solicited, we are informed that photography is strictly forbidden. Their concern for the anonymity and privacy of the scrap metal entering their facility is touching, but while we sit and wait, Durham and I count at least five, possibly seven cameras filming us from every angle. We also talk about how we had both had a very romantic image of ourselves walk- ing amongst the scrap, inspecting shattered remains, and how disap- pointed we are by the reality. The best look I get at the place is just now, using Google Maps "satellite view" to inspect it from orbit.

   Durham is here looking primarily for body parts for his wild boar. The head is already complete and thus far looks fiercely mechanical. Durham tells me, "I wanted him to look the most exotic and powerful that I could make him look." He "wanted to honor the wild-boarness," but also how we respond, "when we see one. We're always shocked by them. Always." He adds, "They make good pets, by the way," describing seeing families who have raised them from birth so that "you see this great giant tusked monster that loves all the children and the children love him." On Durham's boar the long "snout" is twin lengths of threaded pipe extending aggressively side-by-side from the nose cavity, like the double barrels of a shotgun. Or, perhaps, think- ing of their anatomical positioning, like exhaust pipes for mechanical respiration. (In North America, bikers often call their big, rumbling Harley Davidson motorcycles, "hogs.") The pipes and the skull have been spray-painted with a metallic automotive "Chameleon" paint, which looks purple from some angles and turquoise from others. Parts of the skull have been covered in leather that has been painted metallic silver. The right eye is a glass roundel, the left an empty black plastic socket. Durham is skeptical of symmetry and has treated the ears equally differently, although each is some- how convincingly hog-like. The right is a large, brown chunk of accidentally-ear-shaped glass, the subtle molten folds visible in the glass oddly evocative of the folds of skin. The material of the left ear could not be more different: it is a piece of metal screen, thin, but rigid, folded and bent into shape, giving an impression of the fleshy thinness of a boar's ear, when not covered with fur.

Eventually Vollmer returns from his trip into the junkyard with a few items he thinks Durham might be interested in. There are a number of very heavy and precisely machined stainless steel parts: valves, couplings, I'm not sure what, a rusty bit of red-painted heavy pipe and a portion of some sort of sheet metal tank that is, presently at least, open on top. Durham contemplates using the latter for the boar's body, but is not sure about the other parts, although he buys them anyway. Before we leave I snap a few surreptitious photos with my phone, just because.

In the late afternoon on Thursday, Durham and I venture out again, this time by taxi, to the large Bauhaus store in Schöneberg. It sits kitty-corner, across a vast parking lot, from an Ikea. If the word Bauhaus has you imagining a furniture shop or thinking about avant-garde art and design, then you are likely reading this outside of Europe. The image you should be calling to mind is of a large DIY "home & garden center." Durham is especially interested in getting some PVC plastic plumbing pipe and he is delighted to see that Bauhaus has it in a beautiful blue, something he had not expected and calls "a marvelous accident." We collect a few lengths of pipe of different diameters, along with couplings to join them and ninety-degree elbow joints. These will be the body of the Great Dane.

Vollmer is away for the weekend, but Durham is determined to keep gathering body parts. He is especially keen to get furniture for the ibex body, but is also aware that he did not get all the metal he needed for the boar on our trip to the scrapyard. On Saturday, Durham arranges a ride with an artist friend, Brad Downey, who has a friend, Julien, who has a car and can drive us all to the Arena Indoor Flea Market. This is a remarkable place a little northwest of Treptower Park. On the way in, we notice two small brick structures on either side of the street, the nearest of which has a sculpture of a large brown bear on it. I point it out to him and, looking at it, he says, "You can see why my bear has a great big piece of olive wood on top. The shoulders come up way higher than the head."

Inside Durham haggles amicably with a Turkish furniture salesman for two wooden chairs and a small cabinet. He also picks out a metal stair tread with a corrugated surface and an old metal washtub of some sort, which, he says, "is obviously part of a boar's body." Everything fits in the little car except for the washtub, Downey, and me,

so the three of us make our way back to the studio on the S-Bahn.
Downey enjoys contemplating the alchemy by which the modest tub
we are transporting will soon become part of a valuable artwork
and speculates about visiting it in a museum one day. He takes a few
pictures of it on the train to commemorate its ride up in the world.

Back at the studio we begin to break up the furniture into component
parts. If a piece of furniture is hiding secrets, as many do, breaking
it apart will often reveal them. In this case, expensive oak veneer covers
a cheap pine board and "antique"-looking chairs turn out to have
been made using modern joinery techniques. Still, Durham is happy
with the arms and legs, which is what he was after.

Of all the animals Durham is working on, the Great Dane is the
only type I know well from personal experience, although I have seen
moose, bears, and lynx in the wild. My mother, fearful for her safety
while my father was away, decided that what she really needed was,
well, one of the very large animals of Europe. She bought the largest
dog she could find, a tan-colored Great Dane. She named her
Cleopatra, although we called her Cleo for short. As with horses, anyone at child height learned quickly not to walk behind her. She didn't
kick, but if she was happy her wagging tail could quickly whip you
insensible. Her tail (which, like her ears, my mother chose not to crop)
was right at face height for me. Indeed, I have vivid memories of
spending time with Cleo and not being able to see over her back, she
was so tall. She was also gentle and a bit high-strung. Although she
had been spayed, she would occasionally have psychosomatic preg-
nancies that ended with her carrying around and trying to nurse
one of my stuffed toys. I suppose her value as a weaponized dog was
largely in the realm of symbolic deterrence.

Durham's Great Dane body is a heap of parts lying on the floor when
I leave, but later Vollmer sends me a photo of the assembled body,
sans head. Once again, I am stunned at the extent to which the finished
work exceeded my imagination. PVC pipe is challenging to use expressively because of its fixed diameters and the fact that it can only be
joined according to the logic provided by the various elbows and other
couplings, yet despite this I recognize the dog immediately by the
remarkable length of its body and the way this is oddly balanced by
the tall, narrow legs.

Our relationship to animals seems distorted by two conceits. The
first is, as Durham expresses so well, a failure to recognize our kinship.
The other, seemingly paradoxically, is that we often fail to recognize
and respect both their real differences and the human-body situated-
ness of our own forms of thought. Yet, that we see both kinship and
mystery in the faces of other animals is not one of our differences.

As Durham said, we have all experienced animals searching our faces to read our intentions. And we also see both kinship and mystery when we search other human faces ourselves, or even consider our own face in the mirror. I have spent fifty years getting to know myself by observing my own thoughts, emotions, and actions (although it is only the conventions of language that make it seem that these are discrete elements or that I sit aside from them observing), yet many of my own motivations and actions remain mysterious to me. Perhaps it is the recognition of our kinship that creates the space for the kind of careful observing and interacting—and most importantly, observing our interactions—that will open up improved understandings of who we are together in the world.

But this is obviously just a beginning and we should also consider ...

NEUN TAGE UNTER DEN GRÖSSTEN TIEREN EUROPAS

RICHARD WILLIAM HILL

… anschliessend begann Durham, wieder am Braunbärenschädel zu arbeiten. Der Schädel war bereits teilweise mit hellbraunem Gamsleder verkleidet, und auch die Augen waren schon an Ort und Stelle. Als rechtes Auge fungiert eine bräunliche Glaskugel, die von Streifen durchzogen wird. Besonders auffällig ist dabei eine geschwungene schwarze Linie, die zunächst anschwillt, dann einen Winkel von neunzig Grad beschreibt, sich verjüngt und schliesslich ausklingt. Das Glas ist zwar farbig, aber trotzdem halb transparent, es glänzt, hat aber keine Tiefenwirkung. Trotzdem evozieren die schwarzen Wellenlinien den Eindruck einer wilden, fast manischen Energie. Das linke Auge besteht aus einem dunkelbraun-schwarzen, ebenfalls fast opaken, ziemlich unförmigen Glasstück. Die merkwürdige Form des Glasklumpens, den ein Glasbläser auf Murano weggeworfen hat, vermittelt den Eindruck einer leicht gewölbten, nach vorne gerichteten Pupille. Eine hellblaue Wellenlinie verstärkt noch diesen Eindruck einer vorwärtsdrängenden Dynamik. Später hat Durham mir erzählt, dass er Tieraugen nie völlig naturalistisch wiedergebe: «Ich möchte den Tod dieser Tiere zeigen, nicht den Eindruck erwecken, dass sie noch leben würden … obwohl der Tod nicht *so* endgültig ist, wie wir häufig glauben.» Und dann erzählte er mir noch, dass er sich bei der Auswahl des Materials immer frage, «welches Objekt dem toten Tier wohl helfen könnte, besser zu sehen. Aber natürlich würde so ein Tier nicht so sehen, wie lebendige Dinge sehen, deshalb braucht es ein besonderes Auge, das aber unbedingt nicht wie ein echtes Auge aussehen muss.»

Und so bin ich schon einige Minuten später darüber im Bilde, dass der Künstler das Gamsleder zunächst ein paar Stunden in verdünntem Leim eingeweicht und die Flecken dann noch mal von beiden Seiten mit Leim bestrichen hat. Diese Vorgehensweise gestattet es, das Leder wie eine Haut auf den Schädel aufzubringen. Gamsleder stammte früher meist von europäischen Wildgämsen, heute dagegen handelt es sich beim Produkt, das unter diesem Namen verkauft wird, meist um die Haut von Hausschafen oder -ziegen. Ich habe dann zugeschaut, wie Durham nach dieser Methode braune Lederflecken auf der Rückseite des Schädels applizierte. Später hat er noch ein paar Zierleisten aus Holz angebracht, um der Arbeit «eine dezidiert europäische Anmutung» zu geben und dann noch ein paar farbige Glasscherben und Kacheln, die der Arbeit wieder einen etwas anderen Charakter gaben und sie ornamentaler und weniger ungestüm erscheinen liessen. Für den Körper verwendete er ein kräftiges Stück Olivenholz.

Mitten im Satz begonnen habe ich diesen Essay, weil dies meine eigene Begegnung mit Durhams Arbeiten am besten wiedergibt. Der Abgabetermin des Textes ist wegen der noch erforderlichen Übersetzung ins Deutsche und der übrigen Zwänge der Katalogproduktion so festgesetzt, dass ich die Arbeiten, über die ich hier schreibe, in fertigem Zustand gar nicht mehr sehen werde. Allerdings habe ich vereinbart, dass ich Durham bei der Arbeit an diesen Werken in seinem Atelier besuchen kann, und bin deshalb trotz meines engen Terminkalenders Mitte März für neun Tage von Vancouver nach Berlin gefahren. In Berlin war ich fast die ganze Zeit mit Durham zusammen, habe sein Atelier besucht, Fotos und Videos gemacht, mich mit ihm unterhalten und ihm meist einfach bei der Arbeit zugeschaut und beobachtet, wie die Objekte entstehen. Meist waren dabei auch zwei von Durhams Assistenten anwesend: Kai Vollmer, der schon seit ein paar Jahren für Durham tätig ist und ihm bei der Erledigung administrativer Dinge und der Herstellung von Objekten hilft, und William Nicholson, der auf Teilzeitbasis in Durhams Atelier arbeitet und ihm ebenfalls bei der Montage hilft. Während meines Aufenthalts ist Durham vor allem mit der Arbeit am Körper eines Bären beschäftigt. Ein paarmal habe ich auch selbst mitgeholfen – beispielsweise irgendwelche Sachen von A nach B getragen oder bei Bedarf auch mal Holz gesägt. Allerdings war zum Zeitpunkt meiner Abreise noch nichts richtig fertig, aber ich hatte trotzdem den Kopf voller Bilder und Ideen, die ich erst noch verarbeiten musste. Fangen wir also am besten mit dem kulturellen Kontext an.

Der anthropologische Kontext
Dem Leser dürfte bekannt sein, dass es Menschen gibt, die von Tieren nicht nur fasziniert sind, sondern sich ihnen tief verbunden fühlen. Dagegen könnte man einwenden, dass alle Menschen so oder so von Tieren fasziniert sind, und das stimmt natürlich auch. Aber die Leute, die ich hier meine, legen in allen Lebensbereichen eine – wenn man mir diese Verallgemeinerung gestattet – besondere Tierliebe an den Tag. Sie schmücken ihre Kleidung, ihre Wohnung, die Orte, an denen sie sich öffentlich versammeln, mit Tiermotiven, die sie nicht selten als Totem verehren und auf die sie ihre Zugehörigkeit zu einer bestimmten sozialen Gruppe oder zur Kriegerkaste zurückführen. Ja, sie geben sich sogar selbst Namen wie «Wolf», «Adler», «Rabe» oder «Bär», um die besonderen Kräfte und Fähigkeiten, die sie diesen Tieren zuschreiben, für sich zu aktivieren. Manche dieser Menschen – vielleicht sogar die mit den feinsten spirituellen Antennen – stehen mit ihrem Tier sogar in einer ganz persönlichen Beziehung und betrachten es als ein besonderes Mitgeschöpf. Dabei begründen sie ihre besondere Nähe zu einem bestimmten Tier nicht etwa mit wissenschaftlichen Argumenten und stellen manchmal den Charakter eines Tiers sogar falsch dar, damit es besser in ihr mythisches Gesellschaftskonzept passt. Jedenfalls sollten wir uns über diesen kulturellen Kontext im Klaren sein, wenn wir Durhams Projekt verstehen wollen. Ich meine hier natürlich die Europäer.

Im Übrigen möchte ich hier ausdrücklich betonen, dass es sich bei Durhams Projekt um den sehr ernst gemeinten Versuch handelt, sich in den heutigen europäischen Diskurs über die Tiere einzuschalten. Bei seiner Arbeit handelt sich um eine Intervention in diesen Diskurs, die genauso berechtigt ist wie jeder andere intellektuell wertvolle Beitrag. Dennoch handelt es sich nicht um einen Blick von aussen. Durham hat nämlich Jahrzehnte in Europa verbracht und ist ausserdem in einem von europäischen Siedlern geschaffenen Nationalstaat aufgewachsen. Die Arbeiten, die er in dieser Ausstellung zeigt, nötigen uns im Übrigen sogleich dazu, uns mit unserer Beziehung zu den Tieren auseinanderzusetzen. Es geht also um die zahlreichen Widersprüche, mit denen uns die europäische Tradition im Hinblick auf unser Verhältnis zur nicht menschlichen Welt konfrontiert. Seit einiger Zeit kreist diese Diskussion vor allem um den neuen Materialismus, die objektorientierte Ontologie, den Nichtanthropomorphismus und das jüngst ausgerufene Anthropozän. Denn wir begreifen erst langsam, dass diese Systeme der Differenz zwischen Natur und Kultur, domestizierten und wilden Tieren mit einer sowohl faktisch als auch konzeptionell unerhört intensiven Abhängigkeit einhergehen.

Dass die Grösse der Tiere eine so wichtige Rolle spielt, liegt an der europäischen Dimension des Projekts. Bei einigen Tieren ist diese Grösse schlicht ein Ergebnis der Evolution – etwa beim riesigen Elch. Selbst die mächtigen Maremmana-Rinder, die aussehen, als ob sie direkt einer prähistorischen europäischen Höhlenmalerei entsprungen sind, hatten ihre heutige Grösse wohl schon zum Zeitpunkt ihrer Domestizierung erreicht. Andere Tiere, etwa die Deutsche Dogge, hat der Mensch Durham zufolge «so gross gezüchtet, wie es nur ging. Alle anderen Völker haben ebenfalls Hunde, trotzdem haben sie nie daran gedacht, solche Giganten zu züchten. Das ist wirklich eine typisch europäische Idee.» Allerdings, fügt er hinzu, «sind die Hunde immer sehr nett», und man kann sich normalerweise leicht mit ihnen anfreunden. Da er in seiner Arbeit jedoch ihre Grösse thematisiert, lenkt Durham unsere Aufmerksamkeit auf die Frage, nach welchen Kriterien wir Tiere bewerten. Er sagt: «Ich finde, dass Hamster und Maulwürfe und auch viele Mäusearten ganz aussergewöhnliche, ja sehr spezielle Tiere sind, aber die meisten Menschen finden vor allem grosse Tiere beeindruckend und bedeutsam ... dabei sind wir doch in Wirklichkeit allesamt Brüder und Schwestern.»

Schädel
Ich habe gewisse Skrupel, mit den Schädeln zu beginnen, weil man sie so leicht missverstehen kann, aber mir bleibt ja keine Wahl. Der Schädel ist nicht nur der anspruchsvollste Teil der Arbeiten, er bildet auch den Ausgangspunkt des Körpers der Skulpturen. Das war auch im Atelier schon deutlich zu erkennen. Als ich dort eintraf, war der Künstler mit der Gestaltung der meisten Schädel bereits fertig, allerdings hatten sie noch keinen Körper. Der Steinbockschädel war schon mit grossen künstlichen Augen ausgestattet, wie sie der Tierpräparator sonst für einen Elch verwendet. Der Schädel selbst ist grün bemalt. Sein Hals besteht – von hinten nach vorne betrachtet – aus einem Stück Metallrohr, einem Stück einer alten Zierleiste, die der Künstler in Turin erworben hat, und einem relativ neuen – genau wie die Leiste kunstvoll gedrechselten – Tisch- oder Stuhlbein. Fehlt nur noch der Körper, der ebenfalls aus Stuhlelementen bestehen soll, weil es für Durham zwischen dem eleganten Schwung des Geweihs und den anmutigen Biegungen der Stuhlteile eine Verbindung gibt.

Manche der Schädel sind noch nackt und bleiben dies womöglich auch – zum Beispiel der des Moschusochsen. Im Laufe der Woche, am Freitag genau genommen, trifft der – wie ein Kunstwerk in einer Kiste verstaute – Schädel des Maremmana-Bullen ein. Ich öffne die Kiste, nehme den Schädel heraus und lege ihn auf dem Fussboden auf eine Decke. Durham sitzt neben dem Schädel und nimmt ihn in Augenschein. Anders als bei den übrigen Schädeln sind hier schon die Spuren der Zeit, vielleicht sogar der Elemente, zu erkennen. Oben im Schädeldach befindet sich ein kleines Loch: das Einschussloch aus dem Schlachthaus. Als ich von Durham wissen will, was mit ihm passiert, wenn er so einen Schädel zum ersten Mal sieht und anfängt, sich damit zu beschäftigen, antwortet er: «Kann ich nicht so genau sagen, aber ich weiss, dass das Gefühl gar nicht so viel anders ist

als bei einem Lebewesen, das noch am Leben ist. Das kann ein Mensch sein oder ein Gorilla, eine Kuh oder ein Hund, man schaut sich einfach ins Gesicht. Die meisten Tiere mögen es nicht, wenn man sie anstarrt. Wenn man sie für sich einnehmen will, schaut man sie nur kurz an, wendet dann den Blick ab und dreht sich weg. So gewinnt man ihr Vertrauen.» Das Anstarren ist «zwar ein Angriffsmodus, trotzdem schauen wir uns gegenseitig ins Gesicht», um zu verstehen, was mit dem anderen los ist. «Das ist aber eine völlig andere Art, jemanden – ob Mensch oder Tier – anzuschauen, als es die Voyeure im Zoo tun: der Versuch, das andere Lebewesen zu entziffern, wie wir es ja auch bei Menschen tun, wenn wir ihnen ins Gesicht schauen.»

Durham erklärt mir, dass seine Arbeiten, bei denen der Schädel den Ausgangspunkt bildet, den Versuch darstellen, den Geist des betreffenden Tieres zum Ausdruck zu bringen, ihm Achtung zu bezeugen. Das ist eine Feststellung, die man nur allzu leicht missverstehen kann. Da ich Durham inzwischen lange kenne, weiss ich nämlich genau, dass es ihm völlig fernliegt, einen wie immer gearteten indigenen Mystizismus zu kultivieren. Als Autor, der über indigene Kunst (vor allem der Cree) schreibt, möchte ich deshalb an dieser Stelle nur kurz (wirklich nur ganz kurz) darauf hinweisen, dass Durham in seinem Kunstschaffen keine Cherokee-Perspektive einnimmt, obwohl er im Laufe seines Lebens immer wieder auf das intellektuelle Erbe seiner Cherokee-Vorfahren Bezug genommen hat. Wenn er so spricht, möchte er gewiss nicht eine wie auch immer geartete Cherokee-Geheimlehre evozieren, die zwar alles erklärt, die man aber nie wirklich zu fassen bekommt. Durham ist ein zutiefst origineller Denker, der sich ebenso kritisch wie innovativ mit ganz unterschiedlichen kulturellen und intellektuellen Traditionen auseinandergesetzt hat – darunter auch mit seinem eigenen indigenen Kulturerbe. Er steht also durchaus nicht für eine bestimmte Tradition, und gerade das macht ihn so interessant.

Während seines Besuchs habe ich ihn gebeten, mir zu sagen, was für ihn «Geist» («spirit») bedeute. Da ich persönlich nicht so spirituell unterwegs bin, verweist das Wort für mich zunächst einmal ganz allgemein auf den Charakter, die Erscheinung, die Lebensenergie usw. des betreffenden Tieres, auf (s)eine Präsenz, die sich jeder präzisen Definition entzieht. Aus meiner Sicht kann man deshalb über diesen «Geist» ohnehin nur in poetischen Bildern sprechen. Seine Antwort: «Ich möchte alle diese Schädel so schmücken, als ob ich ein Europäer wäre, der Schädel schmückt. Deshalb habe ich auch immer darauf geachtet, dass ich europäische Sachen verwende: Glas, Textilien, Farbe.» Es geht doch nur darum, «den Geist dieses Tiers zurückzubringen, nicht um sein Abbild» im mimetischen Sinne. Wieweit dies gelingt, hängt allerdings von der Bereitschaft des Publikums ab, sich auf diese Idee einzulassen. «Erfolg gibt es in der Kunst doch gar nicht ... vielleicht ist man in einem bestimmten Sinne erfolgreich, aber der wahre Erfolg besteht doch im Zusammenspiel zwischen dem Kunstwerk, dem Künstler und dem Publikum. Mal abwarten.» Die künstlerische Arbeit ist deshalb in der Ausstellung Bestandteil der Kommunikation des Künstlers mit seinen Mitmenschen – oder eine Kommunikation, die uns dabei hilft, herausfinden, was es bedeutet, Mensch *in* der Welt zu sein und nicht bloss ein Mensch, dem es darum geht, die Welt zu transzendieren oder zu beherrschen. Wenn wir, wie es Durham in seinem Kunstschaffen unterstellt, zutiefst mit dem Dasein der Tiere verwoben sind und wenn diese gar nicht so radikal anders sind als wir, dann müssen wir selbst ja auch gar nicht mehr so sein, wie wir uns das bisher vorgestellt haben.

Für Durham ist die Arbeit mit den Schädeln eine Methode, sich mit der moralischen Dimension unserer Beziehung zu den Tieren auseinanderzusetzen. «Wenn ich an diesen Schädeln arbeite, sehe ich ganz klar, dass wir in Wahrheit alle zu derselben Familie gehören. Ich sehe, dass die Tiere genauso einen Schädel haben wie wir, dass ihr Körper *genauso* ist wie unser Körper.» Diese Verwandtschaft ist für uns von grosser Bedeutung, denn: «Jedes Tier reagiert auf menschliche Liebe. Es mag schmalzig klingen, aber das gilt wirklich für jedes Tier. Jedes Tier / Lebewesen wartet sozusagen auf Liebe und Freundschaft, jedes Tier / Lebewesen hofft darauf, dass die Gefahr und der Hunger zwischendurch mal aufhören. Das habe ich schon als Kind verstanden. Und genau deswegen ist es etwas ebenso Grossartiges wie Merkwürdiges, ein Mensch zu sein: ein Privileg, aber auch eine Verantwortung.»

Als ich jetzt zum ersten Mal in Durhams Berliner Atelier komme, hat der riesige Shire-Horse-Schädel schon einen Hals: ein schweres Holzbrett, an dem Holzstücke befestigt sind. Der nackte Schädel hat Ohren aus Holz, und in seiner Nasenhöhle steckt zerknautscht ein Stück Kupferblech. Das Blech erinnert an den dampfenden Atem des Tiers – vielleicht ein Symbol seiner Lebensenergie. Wer je mit Pferden zu tun hatte, kennt die weissen Atemwolken, die sie manchmal ausstossen. Die meisten dieser Details werden jedoch noch vor meiner Abreise wieder geändert. Doch zunächst mal bin ich sehr beeindruckt davon, wie unglaublich wild dieses Pferd aussieht, wie bösartig geradezu. Dieser Eindruck verdankt sich der Form der Augenhöhle selbst und dem Schwung des Stirnbeins, das zusammen mit dem Auge den Eindruck eines hämischen Grinsens erweckt. Auch die aufwärts gebogene Linie des Kiefers wirkt wie ein bösartiges Grinsen. Diese Wirkung hat der Pferdeschädel mit den vielen menschlichen Totenschädeln gemein, die zu grinsen scheinen (wobei es vermutlich sogar der grinsende Schädel ist, der den «Jolly Roger» [den Totenkopf auf der Piratenflagge, d. Übers.] so lustig [«jolly»] erscheinen lässt). Als ich die Schädel ringsum näher betrachtete, stellte ich fest, dass der bedrohliche Schwung des Stirnbeins auch bei anderen grossen Pflanzenfressern zu beobachten ist. Der Bär, der Luchs und die Deutsche Dogge sehen wegen ihres gefährlichen Gebisses sehr bedrohlich aus, die bedrohliche Wirkung der Pflanzenfresser verdankt sich lediglich einem Zufall der Evolution, der zwar etwas über die Anatomie des Tieres, jedoch nichts über seinen Charakter aussagt. Wenn der Schädel solcher Tiere mit Fell und Muskeln umkleidet ist, verfügen sie über mimetische Ausdrucksmittel, die der Mensch wenigstens teilweise zu entschlüsseln vermag. Aber der Künstler muss sich zudem mit dem Umstand auseinandersetzen, dass auch der nackte Knochen eine (mitunter sehr ausgeprägte) zufällige Expressivität besitzen kann. Beim vierhörnigen Schaf Manx Loaghtan – einer Rasse, die auf der Isle of Man heimisch ist – bringt Durham diese Expressivität sogar zur Geltung.

Der Pferdeschädel wird jedoch so beschichtet, als wäre er mit richtigem Fleisch umkleidet, das auch die Augenhöhlen auskleidet und den Kiefer so umschliesst, dass vom furchterregenden Schädel darunter nichts mehr zu sehen ist. Diesen Prozess zu beobachten, ist ausgesprochen interessant. Als ich dazustosse, hat Durham bereits Stücke eines gedrechselten Geländers am Hals und in den seitlichen Kiefermulden befestigt, in denen sonst die Muskeln liegen. Die Geländerstange ist unglaublich gewunden, was mich auf den Gedanken bringt, dass die Dinge, die wir machen, von unserer körperlichen Beschaffenheit beeinflusst sind, und dass andere Strukturen in der Welt an unserem Körper Spuren hinterlassen. Als ich darüber später mit Durham spreche, meint er nur, dass er sich nicht weiter darüber gewundert habe, dass die Windungen der Geländerstange sich zum Teil perfekt an den Kiefer anschmiegten. Kurz darauf sah ich dann zu meinem Erstaunen, wie er viele dieser Teile mit Leder umkleidete. Er begründete die Massnahme damit, dass das Publikum die Stücke sonst ganz nüchtern als «ein Stück Holz» betrachten würde, «das an einem Kiefer befestigt ist», und darüber den Pferdemuskel völlig vergessen würde. Das wollte er unbedingt vermeiden. «Deshalb habe ich die Partien notdürftig mit Leder verkleidet.» Damit wollte der Künstler jedoch nicht etwa den Eindruck von Authentizität zu erwecken, was ihm denkbar fernliegt, vielmehr wollte er durch die Wahl der Materialien den Charakter des Tiers einfangen. Trotzdem sollen die Materialien nicht vortäuschen, etwas zu sein, was sie gar nicht sind –

da Durhams Tierpräparate und die diversen Formen des darstellenden «Realismus» ohnehin nicht leiden –, sondern sich lediglich ins betreffende skulpturale Projekt integrieren.

Körperteile

Wie bereits erwähnt, verdanken die Körper von Durhams Skulpturen ihr Erscheinungsbild vor allem dem Nachdenken über die Schädel. Doch sollten wir uns hier vielleicht zunächst noch mit dem genreübergreifenden Charakter nicht nur dieser Körper, sondern auch der Schädel selbst befassen. Wie die meisten Durham-Skulpturen bestehen sie aus höchst unterschiedlichen «Ingredienzien». Allerdings würde ein Inventar hier auch nicht weiterhelfen. Man könnte sagen, dass jede der hier behandelten Tierskulpturen auf die eine oder andere Weise die folgenden «Ingredienzien» enthält: eine lebenslange Vorliebe für explorative Spaziergänge in den unterschiedlichsten Milieus und Weltgegenden, ob in der Stadt oder auf dem Land; eine lebenslange Vorliebe für den Umgang mit menschlichen oder nicht menschlichen Lebewesen («animals»); eine lebenslange Vorliebe für das Gespräch mit anderen Menschen; ein lebenslanges Interesse an den Texten anderer Autoren und an der Herstellung eigener Prosa- und Lyriktexte, eine lebenslange Begeisterung für das Sammeln, die Erkundung und den Umgang mit Dingen; ein lebenslanges Interesse daran, Dinge zu entdecken, umzufunktionieren, zu bemalen, mit Werkzeugen zu bearbeiten, zusammenzubauen, zu verändern und neu zu arrangieren. Diese zuletzt genannte Aktivität, seine Tätigkeit als Skulpteur, resultiert gewissermassen aus all den anderen. Anders ausgedrückt: Sie resultiert aus der Organisation all dieser genreübergreifenden Erfahrungen und materiellen Objekte im Sinne eines sozialen Nachdenkens über uns selbst und unsere Welt. So bin ich zur Überzeugung gelangt, dass die soziale Dimension eine genauso reale Komponente von Durhams Kunstschaffen ist wie die Holz- und Metallstücke usw. Während meines gesamten Besuchs ist Durham fast pausenlos in Gespräche verwickelt: im Atelier, beim Abendessen, bei einer Flasche Wein nach dem Essen.

Körperteile einkaufen in Berlin
«In den nächsten Tagen», sagt Durham, «muss ich unbedingt mal wieder in den einschlägigen Läden hier in Berlin Tierkörperteile einkaufen gehen.» Als ich ihn verwundert ansehe, erklärt er leichthin (aber sichtlich erfreut, dass er einen Blödmann gefunden hat): «Ich meine natürlich Altkleider- und Hinterhofläden, Flohmärkte und so was ...» Tatsächlich erkenne ich schon bald nach meiner Ankunft, dass Durham darauf brennt, seine Schädel mit einem Körper auszustatten, und überlegt, was er dafür am besten verwenden könnte. Und natürlich gibt es da – wie stets – ein paar Sachen, die er vermutlich schon seit Jahren mit sich herumschleppt: in diesem Fall Glasabfälle aus einer Werkstatt in Murano, Olivenholzstücke aus Apulien, alte Zierleisten aus Turin, Rohrstücke und Möbelteile von weiss Gott woher. Aber er braucht noch viel mehr.

Am Montagnachmittag fährt uns Vollmer zum Humana-Secondhand-Kaufhaus unweit des Frankfurter Tors, das in einem Schaufenster mit der Aufschrift «Erstklassiger Secondhand-Markt» Werbung für sich macht. Durham hält dort Ausschau nach schweren Mänteln und Decken, aus denen sich ein passender Körper für den Elchbullen machen liesse. Das Geschäft hat mehrere Etagen, und es dauert eine Weile, bis wir alle infrage kommenden Abteilungen durchwühlt haben und schliesslich mit einem so mächtigen Stapel Mänteln, Hosen und Decken an der Kasse stehen, dass die arme Frau dort eine Kollegin bitten muss, sich um die Kunden zu kümmern, die das Pech haben, hinter uns anzustehen. Nichts zu machen. So ein Elchbulle ist nun mal ziemlich gross.

Durham möchte den Schädel des Elchbullen wie gesagt unbehandelt lassen, nur dass er den fehlenden Unterkiefer inzwischen durch ein kieferförmiges Stück Holz ersetzt hat. Am Kopf des Tiers fehlt ausserdem eine Schaufel, was nach Auskunft des Menschen, der Durham den Schädel

überlassen hat, daran liegt, dass das Tier bei einer Attacke auf einen Zug ums Leben gekommen ist. Als Durham mir erklärt, wie er sich den Körper des Tiers – eine Ansammlung von Mänteln und Decken – ungefähr vorstellt, kann ich mir nicht recht vorstellen, was er genau meint. Ein paar Tage später schickt Vollmer mir dann jedoch ein Foto der fertigen Arbeit, die einem Elch tatsächlich erstaunlich ähnlich sieht, ohne dass man deswegen auch nur eine Sekunde daran zweifelt, dass es sich natürlich in Wirklichkeit um ein mit Decken und Mänteln umwickeltes Metallgerüst handelt. Den krönenden Abschluss bildet ein Sami-inspirierter Pullover norwegischer Machart.

Am nächsten Tag bin ich – leider völlig grundlos – richtig gespannt. Ich darf Durham nämlich auf einen Schrottplatz begleiten. Dank Hollywood stelle ich mir vor, dass wir zwischen Halden ausgeschlachteter Autos, abgewrackten Riesenmaschinen und anderen faszinierenden Gerätschaften umherspazieren werden, während Durham sich die Sachen aussucht, die er braucht, um vor allem für seinen Keiler einen Körper zu bauen. Als wir dort eintreffen, begehe ich den Fehler, Durham zu filmen, was – wie sich herausstellt – streng verboten ist. Vollmer entschuldigt sich in unserem Namen bei den Leuten dort, doch die haben schon beschlossen, dass wir das Gelände nicht betreten dürfen – aus Haftungsgründen, wie sie sagen. Schliesslich nennen sie uns einen anderen Schrottplatz, der angeblich nicht weit entfernt ist, ziemlich nahe beim S-Bahnhof Schöneberg, sagen sie. Dort angekommen, lasse ich die Kamera gleich im Auto. Dann gehen wir alle drei vorne ins Büro. Dort erfährt Vollmer, dass er – wieder mal aus Haftungsgründen – nur allein auf dem Gelände nach Sachen Ausschau halten darf. Durham und ich müssen am Tor warten, bis er mit den Dingen, die er findet, nach vorne kommt und sie uns zeigt. Ausserdem muss er eine Leuchtweste tragen und – soweit ich es verstehe – unterschreiben, dass er gegenüber den Betreibern keinerlei Ansprüche geltend macht, sollte er während seines Besuchs auf dem Gelände zufällig zerquetscht oder anderweitig ins Jenseits befördert werden. Und auch hier werden wir – ohne dass wir dafür den geringsten Anlass geboten hätten – darauf hingewiesen, dass Fotografieren streng verboten sei. Dass sich die Leute derart um die Anonymität der Schrottteile sorgen, die bei ihnen aufs Gelände gebracht werden, ist ja irgendwie rührend, dabei zählen Durham und ich, während wir vorne am Tor warten, zwischen fünf und sieben Kameras, die uns von allen Seiten filmen. Wir unterhalten uns auch darüber, dass wir uns unseren Schrottplatzbesuch wesentlich romantischer vorgestellt hatten und nun beide ziemlich enttäuscht sind. Die beste Ansicht des Platzes verdanke ich der Google-Maps-Funktion «satellite view», die ich später mal aktiviert habe, um mir den Ort aus dem Weltraum anzusehen.

Durham sucht hier vor allem Körperteile für seinen wilden Keiler. Der Kopf ist bereits komplett und sieht schon ganz schön gefährlich aus. Er sagt: «Ich wollte, dass er so exotisch und kraftvoll wie nur möglich aussieht.» So wollte er «dem Keilersein seine Achtung bekunden», aber auch zeigen, wie wir reagieren, «wenn wir so ein Tier sehen: Wir sind jedes Mal total schockiert, jedes Mal.» Dann sagt er: «So ein Keiler ist übrigens ein nettes Haustier» und erzählt von Familien, die solche Tiere grossgezogen haben, «und dann steht man plötzlich vor so einem Riesenviech mit seinen Hauern, das alle Kinder so lieb hat und umgekehrt genauso». Bei Durham besteht der lange Rüssel des Tiers aus zwei Stücken Rohr mit Gewinde, die wie die Läufe einer Doppelflinte aggressiv aus der Nasenhöhle hervorstossen. Angesichts ihrer anatomischen Position könnte man auch sagen: wie in Metall gegossene Atemschläuche. Die Rohre und der Schädel sind mit einem Metallic-Autolack besprüht, der «Chamäleon» heisst und je nachdem, aus welcher Perspektive man ihn anschaut, mal violett, mal türkisfarben aussieht. Teile des Schädels sind mit silber-metallicfarbenem Leder bezogen. Das rechte Auge besteht aus einer Glasscheibe, das linke aus einer schwarzen Steckdose. Durham ist

kein Symmetriefreund und hat deshalb auch die Ohren unterschiedlich gestaltet, obwohl beide durchaus etwas von einem Schwein haben. Beim rechten handelt es sich um ein grosses braunes, zufällig ohrförmiges Stück Glas, dessen Schmelzfalten tatsächlich irgendwie an Hautfalten erinnern. Das linke Ohr besteht aus einem völlig anderen Material: einem dünnen, aber stabilen Stück Blech, das so gebogen ist, dass es buchstäblich an ein nacktes Keilerohr erinnert.

Schliesslich kehrt Vollmer von seinem Schrottplatzbesuch zurück und schleppt ein paar Sachen an, für die Durham sich vielleicht interessieren könnte. Er bringt unter anderem ein paar sorgfältig gearbeitete Edelmetallteile mit: Ventile, Kupplungen, Ich-weiss-nicht-was, ein dickes, schon verrostetes rotes Rohr und einen oben offenen Blechtank. Durham überlegt, ob er aus dem Tank den Körper des Keilers machen soll. Er weiss zwar nicht recht, was er mit den anderen Teilen anfangen soll, kauft sie aber trotzdem. Bevor wir gehen, mache ich mit dem Handy noch schnell ein paar Fotos, nur so zum Trotz.

Am Donnerstag machen Durham und ich uns dann am späten Nachmittag wieder auf den Weg, diesmal mit dem Taxi, und fahren zum grossen Bauhaus-Markt in Schöneberg. Der Markt hat einen riesigen Parkplatz, an den auf der anderen Seite Ikea angrenzt. Das «Bauhaus» ist jedoch nicht etwa ein Laden für Avantgarde-Möbel oder -Design, sondern ein grosser Baumarkt. Durham hofft, dort vor allem ein paar PVC-Plastikrohre zu finden, und ist hocherfreut, dass es sogar Rohre in einem wundervollen Blau gibt – ein Umstand, mit dem er gar nicht gerechnet hatte und den er einen «wundervollen Zufall» nennt. Wir nehmen ein paar von den Rohren in verschiedenen Stärken mit, dazu noch ein paar Verbindungsmuffen und Ellbogenverbinder. Aus diesen Bestandteilen wird der Körper der Deutschen Dogge entstehen.

Vollmer ist übers Wochenende nicht da, was Durham jedoch nicht daran hindert, weiter nach Körperteilen Ausschau zu halten. Dabei hat er es zwar besonders auf Teile für den Steinbockkörper abgesehen, doch gleichzeitig ist ihm klar, dass wir auf dem Schrottplatz nicht alles bekommen haben, was er für den Keiler braucht. Am Samstag organisiert er dann eine Beschaffungstour mit seinem Künstler-Freund Brad Downey, dessen Freund Julien ein Auto hat und uns zum Hallenflohmarkt in der Arena Treptow fahren kann. Das ist ein bemerkenswerter Ort unweit des Treptower Parks. Als wir dort aufs Gelände gehen, sehen wir rechts und links der Strasse je einen kleinen Backsteinbau. Oben auf einem der Sockel ist die Skulptur eines grossen braunen Bären zu sehen. Ich mache Durham darauf aufmerksam, und als er den Bären sieht, sagte er. «Jetzt verstehst du vielleicht, warum ich meinen Bären oben mit einem dicken Stück Olivenholz ausgestattet habe. Die Schultern sind nämlich viel höher als der Kopf.»

In der Halle feilscht Durham freundschaftlich mit einem türkischen Möbelhändler um zwei Holzstühle und ein Schränkchen. Ausserdem wählt er eine Metalltrittleiter und eine alte Blechwanne, «die ich als Körper des Keilers verwende», sagt er. Bis auf den Waschzuber, Downey und mich passt alles ins kleine Auto, also fahren wir mit der S-Bahn zu dritt wieder zum Atelier. Downey stellt unterwegs Betrachtungen darüber an, dass die Wanne, mit der wir unterwegs sind, schon bald Teil eines bedeutenden Kunstwerks sein wird, das man vielleicht eines Tages sogar im Museum bewundern kann. Dann macht er in der S-Bahn noch ein paar Fotos vom Zuber, um den historischen Transport für die Nachwelt festzuhalten.

Im Atelier zerlegen wir später die Möbel in ihre Bestandteile. Wenn ein Möbel ein Geheimnis verbirgt, so kommt dieses spätestens zutage, wenn man das Stück auseinandernimmt. In diesem Fall verbirgt sich unter dem teuren Eichenfurnier billiges Kiefernholz, und die «antiken» Stühle sind bereits das Produkt durchaus moderner Fertigungsverfahren. Trotzdem freut sich Durham über die Stuhlbeine und Armlehnen, die für seine Zwecke genau das Richtige sind.

Nur mit einem der Tiere, an denen Durham arbeitet, habe ich persönlich nähere Erfahrungen gemacht, und zwar mit der Deutschen Dogge, obwohl ich in freier Natur auch schon Elche, Bären und Luchse gesehen habe. Denn meine Mutter, die Angst hatte, wenn mein Vater nicht da war, wollte unbedingt einen dieser grossen europäischen Hunde haben. Und so schleppte sie eines Tages den grössten Hund an, den sie finden konnte: eine hellbraune Deutsche Dogge. Sie nannte das Tier Cleopatra, woraus dann im Alltag Cleo wurde. Wir Kinder lernten schnell, dass es – ebenso wenig wie bei einem Pferd – nicht ratsam war, uns hinter ihr aufzuhalten. Sie schlug zwar nicht mit den Hinterbeinen aus, wedelte aber – wenn sie sich freute – so heftig mit dem Schwanz, dass ein Schlag genügte, um ein Kind ausser Gefecht zu setzen. Ihr Schwanz (den meine Mutter ebenso wenig kupieren liess wie ihre Ohren) befand sich für mich genau auf Kopfhöhe. Tatsächlich erinnere ich mich noch gut daran, dass Cleo sich oft wie eine Barriere in mein Blickfeld schob, dass ich nicht über sie hinwegschauen konnte, so gross war sie. Sie war sehr lieb und ein bisschen nervenschwach. Obwohl sie sterilisiert war, hatte sie manchmal eine Scheinschwangerschaft, was dazu führte, dass sie irgendwann anfing, meine Stofftiere herumzutragen und zu bemuttern. Dagegen bestand ihr Wert als Wachhund vermutlich einzig in ihrer abschreckenden Grösse.

Bei meiner Abreise besteht Durhams grosse Deutsche Dogge einzig aus einem Haufen diverser gebrauchter Bauteile, aber später schickt mir Vollmer ein Foto des zusammenmontierten Körpers, ohne Kopf. Auch hier übertrifft die fertige Arbeit mal wieder bei weitem mein anfängliches Vorstellungsvermögen. Aus PVC-Rohren ein expressives Gebilde zu schaffen, ist wegen ihrer Normierung nicht ganz einfach, aber auch weil man sich dabei nach jener Logik zu richten hat, die durch ihre Verbindungsteile – Muffen und Ellbogenverbindungen – vorgegeben ist. Trotzdem erkenne ich den Hund augenblicklich an seinem auffällig langen Körper und an der Art und Weise, wie er auf seinen hohen dünnen Beinen steht.

Unser Verhältnis zu den Tieren ist durch zwei Fehlannahmen gestört: erstens durch unser Unvermögen, unsere Verwandtschaft mit ihnen zu erkennen, wie Durham es so schön ausgedrückt hat. Zweitens verstehen und respektieren wir jene Differenz, die tatsächlich zwischen ihnen und uns besteht, paradoxerweise gerade nicht, ebenso wenig die durch unseren menschlichen Körper bedingte Form unseres Denkens. Die Erfahrung, dass uns aus dem Gesicht anderer Lebewesen sowohl Verwandtes/Vertrautes als auch völlig Fremdes entgegenblickt, gehört nicht zu jenen Unterschieden. Wie Durham sagt, kennen wir es alle, dass uns ein Tier ins Gesicht blickt, um unsere Absichten zu erraten. Und auch wir selbst begegnen Verwandtem wie Fremdem gleichermassen, wenn wir ins Gesicht anderer Menschen blicken oder sogar, wenn wir uns selbst im Spiegel anschauen. Ich verbringe schon fünfzig Jahre damit, mich selbst kennen zu lernen, indem ich meine eigenen Gedanken, Gefühle und Verhaltensweisen beobachte (obwohl es natürlich nur ein durch die Konventionen der Sprache bedingter Trugschluss ist, dass es sich bei alldem um verschiedene Dinge handelt und dass *ich* von dem getrennt bin, was ich beobachte), trotzdem bleiben mir viele meiner Motive und Verhaltensweisen selbst ein Rätsel. Vielleicht ist es unsere Verwandtschaft, die jenen Raum schafft, dessen wir bedürfen, um sorgfältig zu beobachten und zu interagieren (und vor allem, um unsere Interaktionen sorgfältig zu beobachten) und besser zu verstehen, wer wir alle gemeinsam in dieser Welt sind.

Aber das ist natürlich nur ein Anfang, und wir sollten stets bedenken ...

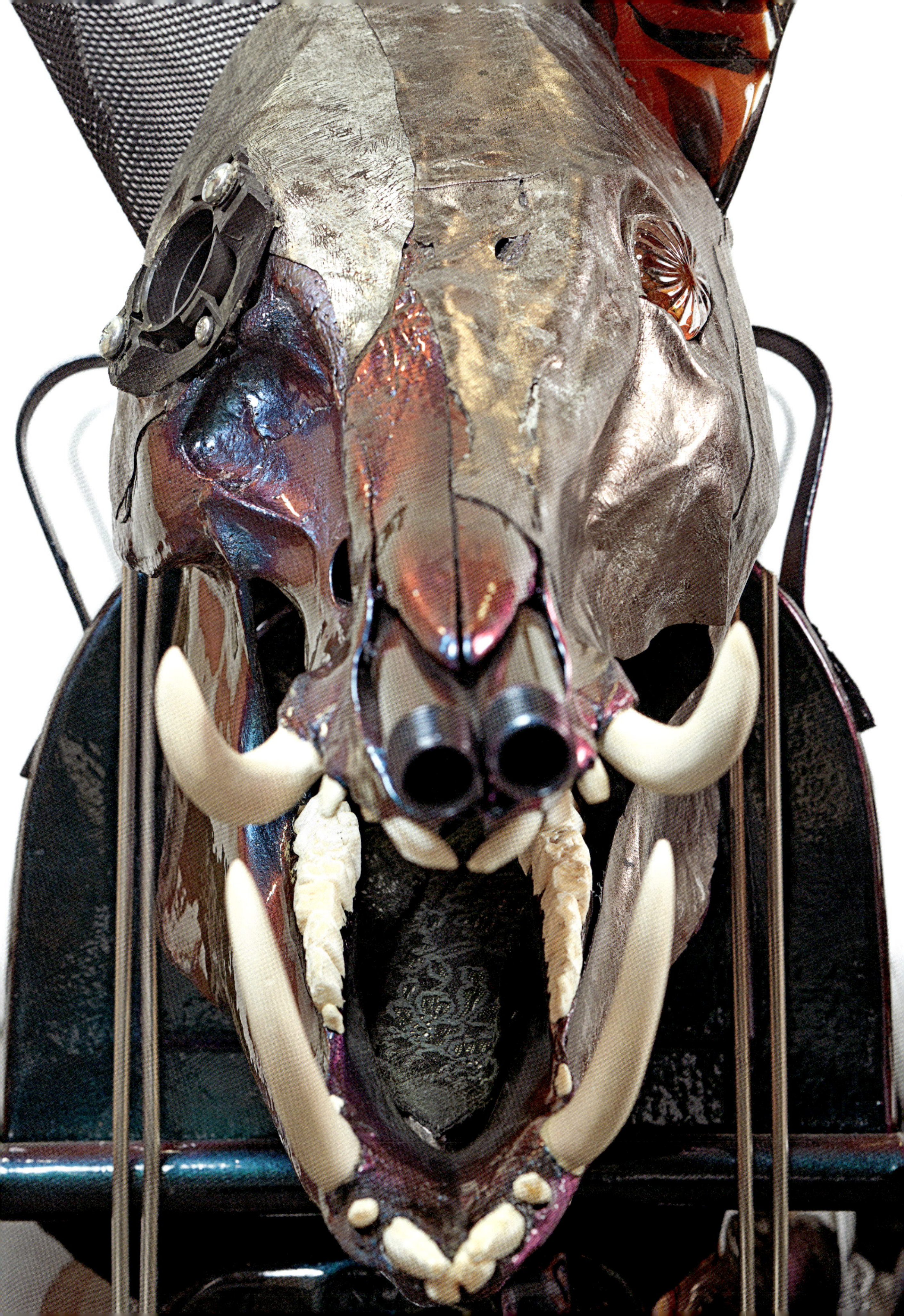

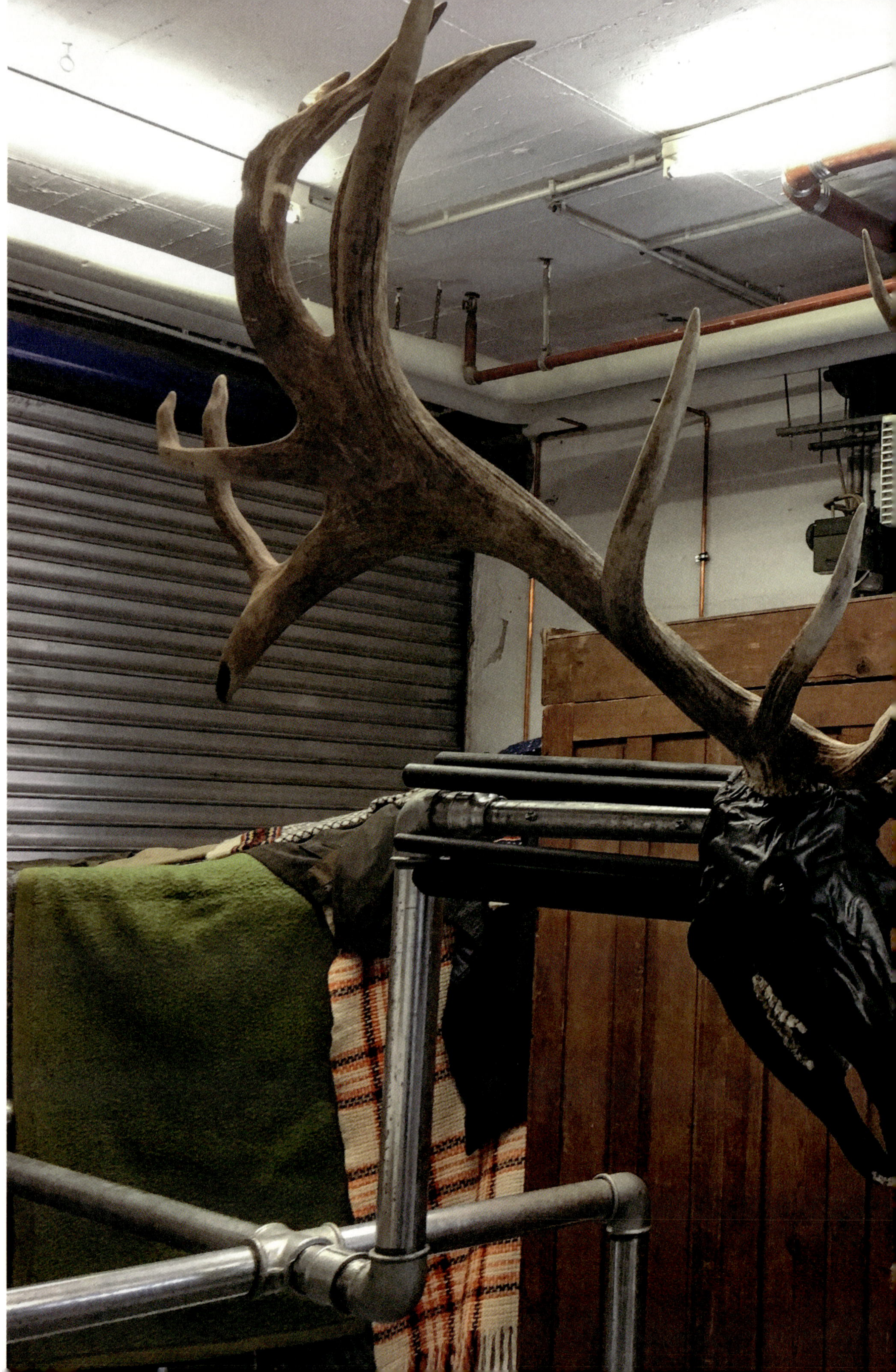

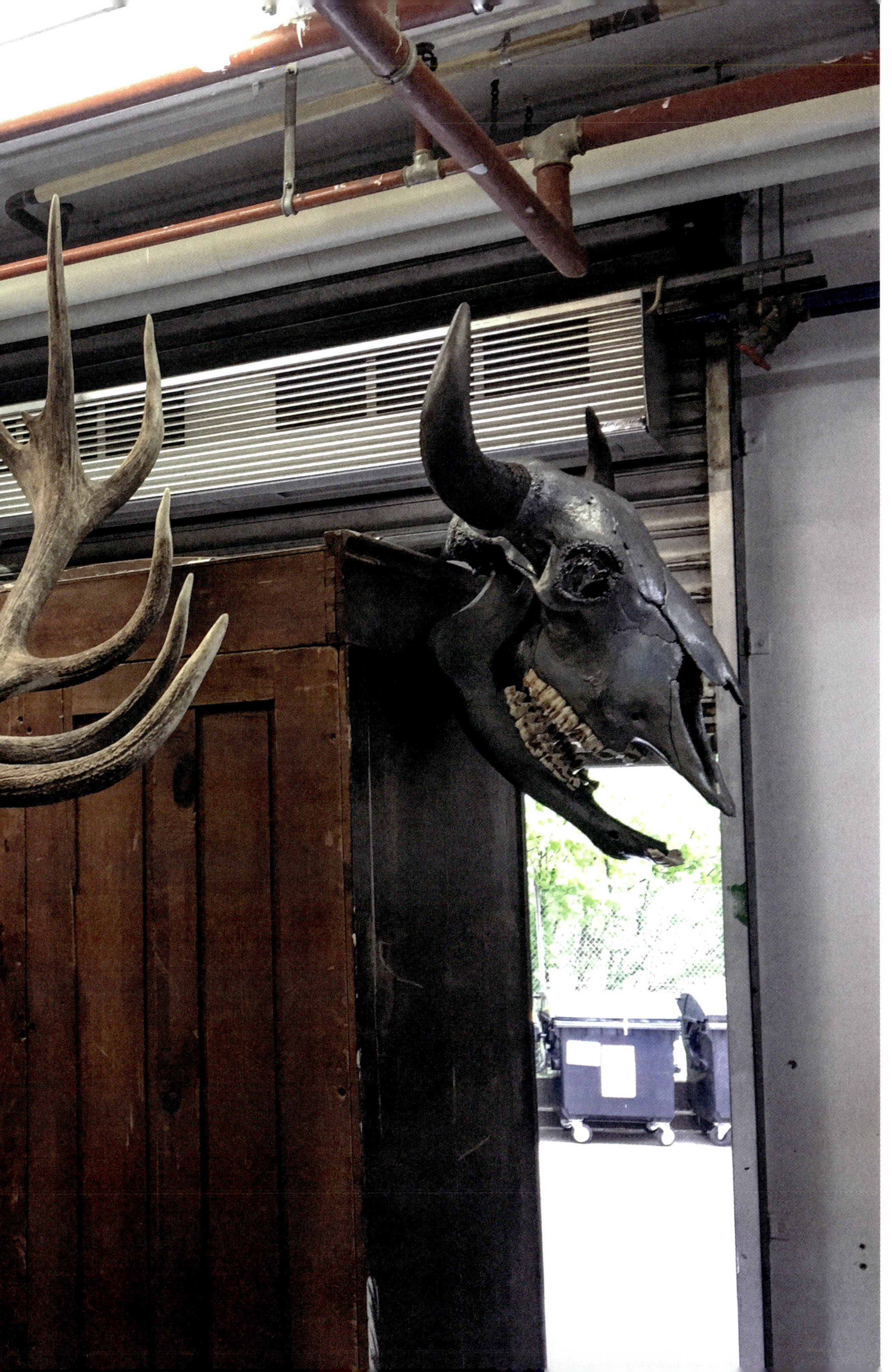

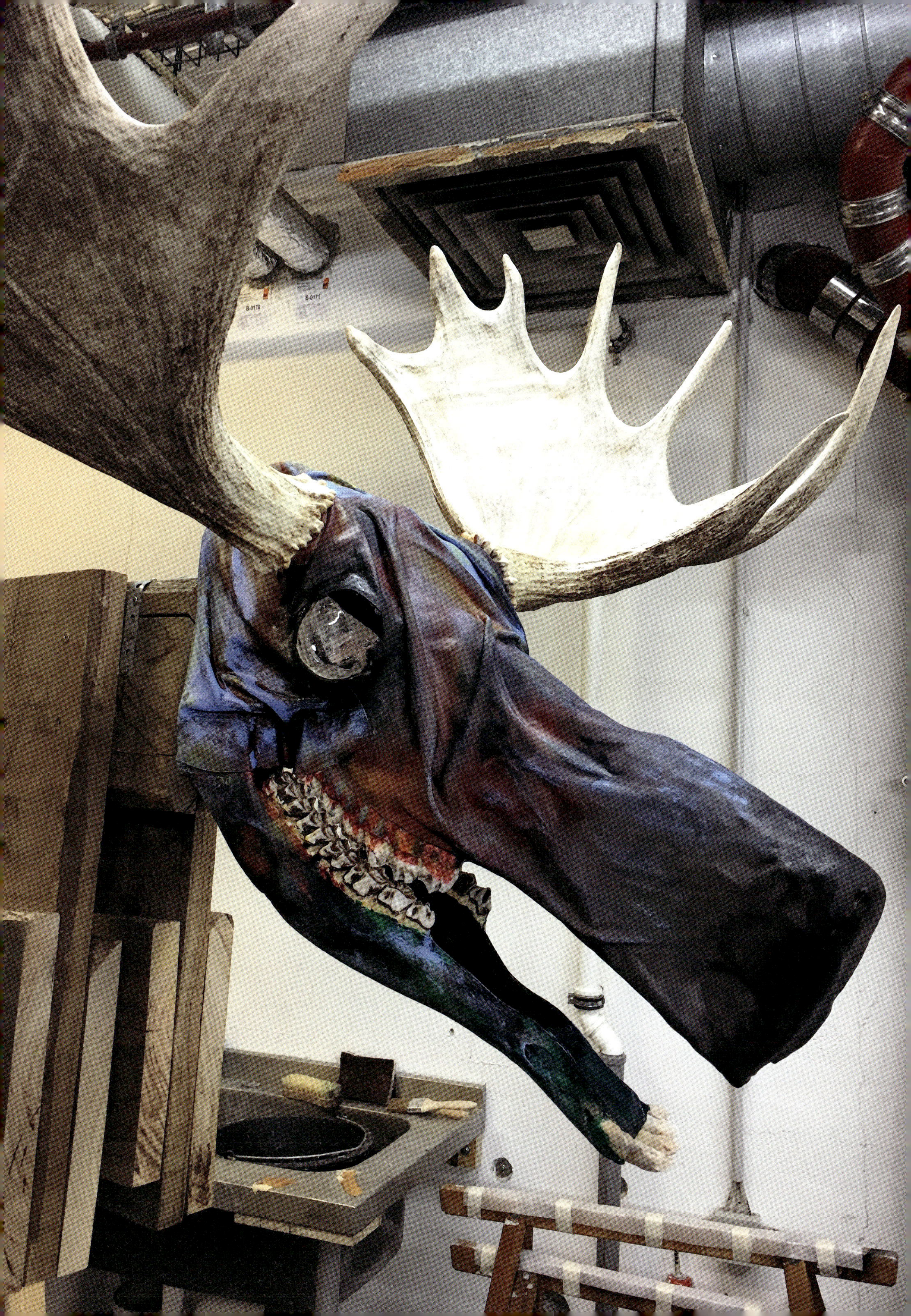

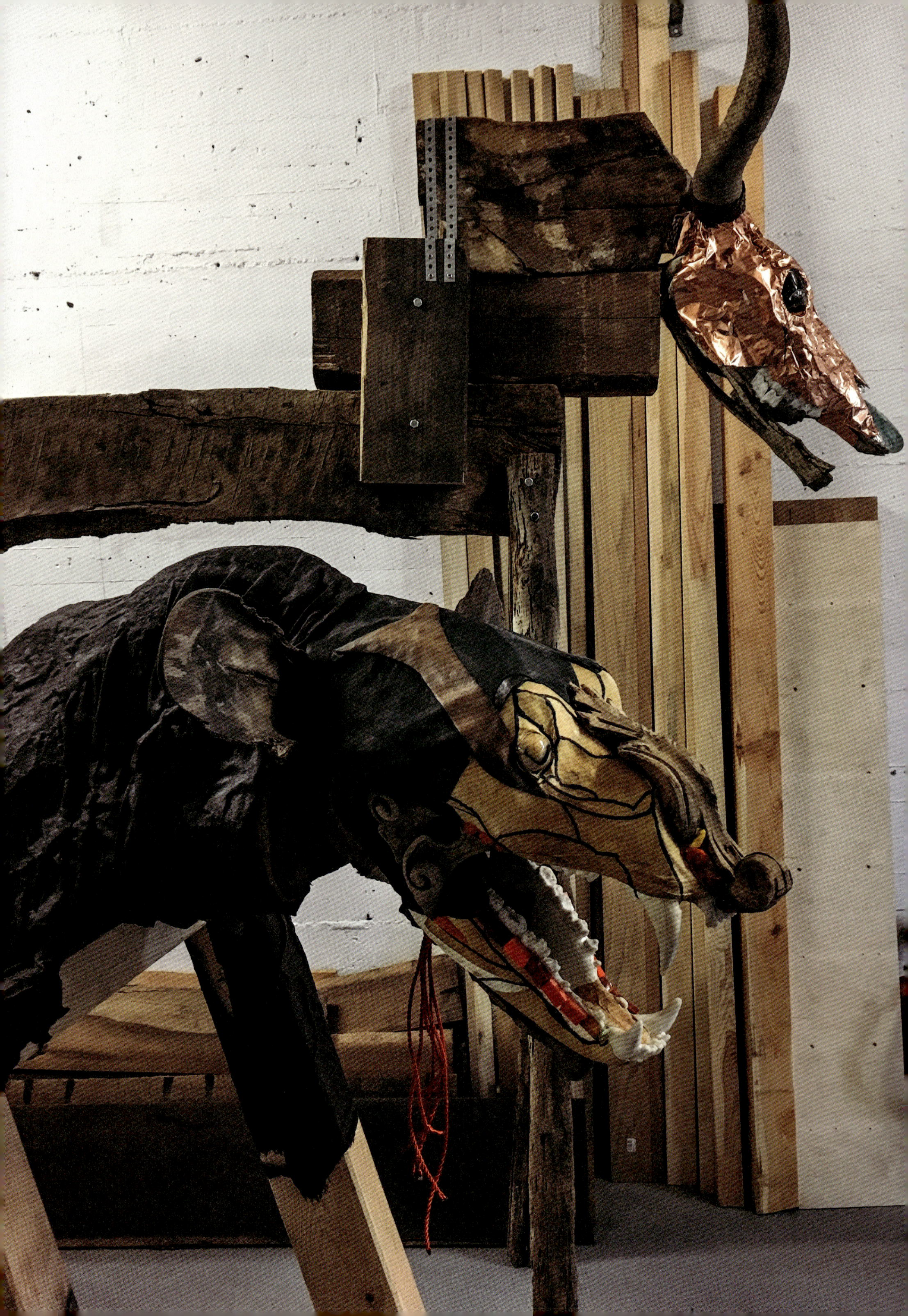

LIST OF WORKS
/
REGISTER OF ANIMALS

Alpine Ibex
Bison / Wisent
Brown Bear
Great Dane
Elk
Eurasian Lynx
Manx Loaghtan
Maremmana Bull
Musk Ox
Reindeer
Red Deer
Shire Horse
Wild Boar
Wolf

Photography:
Nick Ash (unless other stated);
Wilma Lukatsch (3–4, 8, 92–93, 95–96,
back cover), William Nicholson (cover)

All works: Courtesy of the artist

REGISTER OF ANIMALS

Alpine Ibex
The Alpine ibex is a species of goat that is native to the Alps. Remnants excavated in Austria show that the Alpine ibex has lived in the area for at least 3,300 years. In the mountains, it occupies the elevations between the tree line and the ice zone. By the early nineteenth century, human predation had reduced the entire Alpine population to around 100 specimens. Thanks to a successful reintroduction program that drew on this residual stock, the Alpine ibex can now be found in large parts of its historical range. All ibex living in the Alps today are descended from those 100 animals.

Bison / Wisent
The bison is a wild bovine that originally ranged throughout the Northern Hemisphere. The species has divided into two subspecies, the North American bison and its European relative, the wisent. By the 1920s, the wisent was almost extinct. All specimens living today are descendants of only twelve wisents that were kept in zoos and enclosures.

Brown Bear
One of the earth's largest terrestrial carnivores, the brown bear figures prominently in numere ous myths and legends. But humans also saw the animal, correctly or not, as a competitor for scarce resources and a potential threat, and so the species was decimated or extirpated in many areas. The oldest known fossil record of a brown bear was found at a prehistoric hunters' campground in Tyrol and dates from around 5000 BCE. Sizable populations persist in Scandinavia.

Great Dane
The pedigree of the Great Dane can be traced back to dog breeds known in antiquity or even early history. Complete genealogical records go back to the sixteenth century, when Great Danes were kept at princely courts and used to hunt bear, boar, and deer. The tallest dog of all time was a Great Dane called Zeus, which stood 111.8 centimeters (paw to shoulder). In the breed standard, the Great Dane is described as friendly, affectionate, and devoted.

Elk
The elk is the largest extant species of deer and primarily lives in North America, northern Asia, and northern Europe. Unlike most deer species, this herbivore is a solitary animal and prefers to stay within a familiar territory. Its natural predators are the brown bear and the wolf; humans have hunted elk since the Stone Age.

Eurasian Lynx
After the bear and the wolf, the lynx is Europe's third-largest indigenous carnivore. For many decades it was the target of deliberate extirpation efforts, and so the species disappeared from Western Europe until, after around 1950, it migrated back from neighboring areas; there have also been reintroduction schemes. The total European population is currently estimated to number around 7,000 animals.

Manx Loaghtan
This four-horned sheep is native to the Isle of Man. It is a primitive sheep race that, rather than having been bred for commercial purposes, adapted to its natural environment over the course of centuries. By the 1950s, the Manx Loaghtan was nearly extinct. A breeding prod gram has brought the population back up to roughly 1,500 females, but the variety is still considered at risk because it is ill suited to the market's demands (rapid growth, white wool).

Maremmana Bull
The Maremmana is a breed of domestic cattle reared on the steppes of the Maremma, a region in southern Tuscany and northern Lazio. Its robust constitution, longevity, and resistance to illnesses make it especially suitable to this formerly malaria-infested area. The original line of the Maremmana, the Maremmana primitivo, evinces many characteristics of the extinct aurochs, the wild ancestor of domestic cattle. It is bred primarily as a draught animal and for meat.

Musk Ox
Sizable numbers of musk oxen now live in Greenland, Canada, Siberia, and Alaska; smaller herds exist in Norway and Sweden. The animal's preferred habitat is the low-precipitation tundra of the Arctic zone. Unlike reindeer, musk oxen do not migrate across larger distances, instead slowly roaming their territories day after day. The musk ox is currently not considered endangered.

Reindeer
Reindeer inhabit the circumpolar region in northern Eurasia and North America, making them one of the world's northernmost large mammal species. To escape the Arctic winter, the herbivorous animals undertake extensive migrations wherever possible, covering distances of up to 5,000 kilometers. They are the only species of deer to have been domesticated. Reindeer husbandry spread from Siberia to Scandinavia around 1000 BCE, and is still the basis of existence for several indigenous peoples, especially in Siberia and among the Sami.

Red Deer
The red deer stands out among the deer spet cies for its unusually large and highly branched antlers. In Central Europe, the red deer is one of the largest animals living in the wild. It prefers habitats with a closely spaced mixture of structurally diverse forests, thickets, and large open clearings, and so the dense human settlement of the continent's heart has ousted it from much of its erstwhile range. Deer appear in the mythology of numerous European as well as non-European peoples.

Shire Horse
The Shire Horse is a cold-blooded breed and, with a maximum weight of more than 1,200 kilograms and a height at withers averaging 1.78 meters, it is the world's largest horse. Originally bred for use in battle, it later found its true destiny in agriculture and as a draught horse harnessed to England's brewer's drays. Best known for its ability to pull enormous weights, the Shire horse was used in transportation more generally until the advent of motor-powered vehicles; in the early twentieth century, for example, it pulled trams in London.

Wild Boar
Thanks to their adaptability, wild boars now live virtually all over the world. They have been a popular game from time immemorial. In Central Europe, the population is currently surging, primarily because of the growing cultivation of corn, which is also why the animals are increasingly migrating into populated areas. The wild boar is the ancestor of the pig, whose domestication began as early as the eighth millennium BCE.

Wolf
The wolf is the largest carnivore in the canid family and the primitive form of the domestic dog. Until the emergence of agriculture and pastoral farming, it was the world's most widely distributed terrestrial mammal. Since the late Pleistocene, various subspecies ranged throughout Europe, large parts of Asia including the Arabian Peninsula and Japan, and North America. Systematic persecution of the wolf in Central Europe began in the fifteenth century. The population is now gradually recovering in a few isolated areas on the continent.

Compiled by Lea Altner
Sources: Wikipedia, WWF, NABU

TIERREGISTER

Alpensteinbock
Der Alpensteinbock ist eine in den Alpen verbreitete Art der Ziegen. Archäologische Funde in Österreich belegen, dass der Alpensteinbock seit mindestens 3300 Jahren dort angesiedelt ist. In den Alpen lebt er auf der Höhe zwischen Wald- und Eisgrenze. Anfang des 19. Jahrhunderts war die Art im gesamten Alpenraum bis auf etwa 100 Tiere ausgerottet. Dank eines erfolgreichen Wiederansiedlungsprogramms aus diesem Restbestand ist der Alpensteinbock inzwischen wieder in weiten Teilen seines ursprünglichen Lebensraums verbreitet. Alle heute in den Alpen lebenden Steinböcke stammen von diesen 100 Tieren ab.

Europäischer Bison / Wisent
Der Bison ist ein ursprünglich auf der gesamten Nordhalbkugel verbreitetes Wildrind. Mittlerweile hat sich die Art in zwei Unterarten geteilt: die nordamerikanischen Bisons und ihre europäischen Vertreter, die Wisente. In den 1920er Jahren waren die Wisente in Europa akut vom Aussterben bedroht. Alle heute noch lebenden Wisente stammen von nur zwölf in Zoos und Tiergehegen gepflegten Wisenten ab.

Braunbär
Als eines der grössten an Land lebenden Raubtiere der Erde spielt der Braunbär in zahlreichen Mythen und Sagen eine wichtige Rolle, gleichzeitig wurde er als (zumindest vermeintlicher) Nahrungskonkurrent und potenzieller Gefährder des Menschen vielerorts dezimiert oder ausgerottet. Die bisher ältesten bekannten Braunbärbelege stammen von einer prähistorischen Jägerraststelle aus Tirol, datiert auf circa 5000 v. Chr. Grössere Bestände gibt es heute noch in Skandinavien.

Deutsche Dogge
Die Herkunft der Deutschen Dogge ist auf antike oder gar frühgeschichtliche Hundetypen zurückzuführen. Seit dem 16. Jahrhundert lässt sich die Geschichte dieser Hunderasse lückenlos verfolgen. Zu dieser Zeit wurde sie als Bären-, Eber- und Hirschhund an Fürstenhöfen für die Jagd gehalten. Der grösste Hund aller Zeiten war eine Deutsche Dogge namens Zeus, die 111,8 Zentimeter hoch war (Pfote bis Schulter). Im Rassestandard der Deutschen Dogge wird ihr Wesen als freundlich, liebevoll und anhänglich beschrieben.

Elch
Der Elch ist die grösste heutige Art der Hirsche und ist vornehmlich in Nordamerika, Nordasien und Nordeuropa verbreitet. Der Pflanzenfresser ist im Gegensatz zu den meisten anderen Hirscharten Einzelgänger und hält sich in der Regel in einem Gebiet auf, das ihm vertraut ist. Seine natürlichen Feinde sind Braunbären, Wölfe und bereits seit der Steinzeit auch der Mensch.

Eurasischer Luchs
Nach dem Bären und dem Wolf ist der Luchs das drittgrösste Raubtier, das in Europa heimisch ist. Über viele Jahrzehnte wurde der Luchs mit gezielten Ausrottungsmassnahmen verfolgt, sodass die Art aus Westeuropa verschwunden war, bis sie ab etwa 1950 aus angrenzenden Siedlungsgebieten, insbesondere aus Tschechien, wieder einwanderte und auch wieder angesiedelt wurde. Der Gesamtbestand in Europa wird zurzeit auf etwa 7000 Luchse geschätzt

Manx Loaghtan
Das vierhörnige Schaf ist auf der Isle of Man beheimatet. Es gehört zu den primitiven Schafrassen, die sich ohne kommerzielle Schafzucht über Jahrhunderte an ihre Landschaft anpassen konnten. In den 1950er Jahren war die Manx Loaghtan beinahe ausgestorben. Mittlerweile gibt es wieder circa 1500 Muttertiere aus Züchtung – trotzdem ist die Rasse noch immer gefährdet, da sie den kommerziellen Anforderungen (schnelles Wachstum, weisses Fell) nicht entspricht.

Maremmaner Bulle
Die Maremmaner sind eine Hausrindrasse, die in den Grassteppen der Maremmen in der südlichen Toskana und dem nördlichen Latium aufgezogen werden. Aufgrund ihrer Konstitution, Genügsamkeit, Langlebigkeit, und Widerstandsfähigkeit gegen Krankheiten eigneten sie sich besonders für diese ehemals mit Malaria verseuchten Gebiete. Die ursprüngliche Linie des Maremmana, das Maremmana primitivo, weist viele Merkmale des ausgerotteten Auerochsen auf – der Wildform der Hausrinder. Die Rinder werden hauptsächlich als Zugtiere und für ihr Fleisch gezüchtet.

Moschusochsen
Heute leben Moschusochsen in grösserer Zahl in Grönland, Kanada, Sibirien und Alaska sowie als kleinere Herden in Norwegen und Schweden. Sie bevorzugen als Lebensraum die niederschlagsarmen Tundren der Arktis. Anders als Rentiere unternehmen Moschusochsen keine grossen Wanderungen, sondern durchziehen täglich langsam ihr Revier. Moschusochsen gelten gegenwärtig nicht als bedroht.

Rentier
Das Rentier lebt zirkumpolar in Nordeurasien und Nordamerika und zählt damit zu den am weitesten nördlich lebenden Grosssäugern. Um dem arktischen Winter zu entgehen, unternehmen die Pflanzenfresser, wo immer dies möglich ist, grosse Wanderungen – manche bis zu 5000 Kilometern. Es ist die einzige Hirschart, die domestiziert wurde. Die Nutzung des Rens verbreitete sich um etwa 1000 v. Chr. von Sibirien nach Skandinavien und bildet noch heute für einige indigene Völker, vor allem in Sibirien und bei den Samen, die Lebensgrundlage.

Rothirsch
Unter den Hirscharten zeichnet sich der Rothirsch durch ein besonders grosses und weit verzweigtes Geweih aus. Im mitteleuropäischen Raum ist der Rothirsch eines der grössten freilebenden Wildtiere. Sie bevorzugen Lebensräume mit einer engen Verzahnung aus strukturreichen Wäldern, Dickungen, und grossen offenen Lichtungen. In Mitteleuropa ist daher die freie Lebensraumwahl aufgrund der dichten Besiedelung durch den Menschen stark eingeschränkt. Hirsche tauchen in der Mythologie zahlreicher europäischer und aussereuropäischer Völker auf.

Shire Horse
Das Shire Horse ist ein Kaltblutpferd und mit einem maximalen Gewicht von mehr als 1200 Kilogramm sowie einer Widerristhöhe von durchschnittlich 1,78 Meter die grösste Pferderasse der Welt. Ursprünglich als Ritterpferd gezüchtet, fand es seinen eigentlichen Verwendungszweck später in der Landwirtschaft oder auch als Kutschpferd vor den Wagen der englischen Brauereien. Diese Pferde sind vor allem für ihre Fähigkeit bekannt, enorme Gewichte ziehen zu können. Vor der Entwicklung motorisierter Fahrzeuge wurde das Shire Horse auch als Zugtier im Transportwesen eingesetzt – beispielsweise Anfang des 20. Jahrhunderts für die Londoner Strassenbahn.

Wildschwein
Dank ihrer extremen Anpassungsfähigkeit sind Wildschweine inzwischen fast weltweit verbreitet und bereits seit Urzeiten beliebtes Jagdwild. In Mitteleuropa nimmt die Population vor allem durch den vermehrten Anbau von Mais derzeit stark zu. Die Tiere wandern daher auch verstärkt in besiedelte Bereiche ein. Das Wildschwein ist die Stammform des Hausschweins. Die Domestikation des Wildschweins begann bereits im 8. Jahrtausend v. Chr.

Wolf
Der Wolf ist das grösste Raubtier aus der Familie der Hunde und die Stammform des Haushunds. Bis zur Entwicklung der Land- und Weidewirtschaft war es das am weitesten verbreitete Landsäugetier der Welt. Seit dem späten Pleistozän war die Art in mehreren Unterarten in ganz Europa, in weiten Teilen Asiens – einschliesslich der Arabischen Halbinsel sowie Japans – und in Nordamerika verbreitet. Bereits seit dem 15. Jahrhundert wurden Wölfe in Mitteleuropa systematisch verfolgt und ausgerottet. Heute gibt es in Europa vereinzelte Erholungen der Bestände.

Zusammengestellt von Lea Altner
Quellen: Wikipedia, WWF, NABU

Jimmie Durham
Artist, activist, and writer (b. 1940, US)
active in the Civil Rights Movement in the
US, as well as in the American Indian Movement, for which he served as a representative to the United Nations. Durham had
his first solo show in 1965. Since that
time, he has had numerous solo exhibitions, including at the Hammer Museum,
Los Angeles, the Walker Art Center,
Minneapolis, and the Whitney Art Museum,
New York (all 2017). Durham has participated in numerous biennials, including the
Venice Biennale (2012, 2005, 2003, 2001,
and 1999), Bienal de São Paulo (2010),
Biennale de Lyon (2009), Taipei Biennial
(2012), and Biennale of Sydney (2004).
He also participated in documenta 9 (1992)
and (d)OCUMENTA 13 (2012). His writings
have been published in various books and
journals such as *Artforum*, *Third Text*,
and *Black Scholar*. He has lived in Europe
since 1994.

Richard William Hill
Canada Research Chair in Indigenous Studies at Emily Carr University of Art and
Design, Vancouver, Canada. Hill taught
full-time in the art history program at York
University, beginning in 2007 and leaving
as associate professor in 2015. As a curator
at the Art Gallery of Ontario, he oversaw
the museum's first substantial effort to
include Indigenous North American art and
ideas in permanent collection galleries.
He co-curated, with Jimmie Durham, *The
American West* at Compton Verney, UK,
in 2005 and, beginning in 2006, *The World
Upside Down,* which originated at the Walter
Phillips Gallery at the Banff Centre and
toured across Canada. Hill's essays on art
have appeared internationally in numerous
books, exhibition catalogues, and periodi-
cals. He currently has a regular column at
canadianart.ca and is on the editorial board
of the journal *Third Text.*

Heike Munder
Director of the Migros Museum für Gegenwartskunst in Zurich since 2001. While
completing a degree in cultural studies
at the University of Lüneburg, Munder
co-founded the Halle für Kunst Lüneburg
e. V., which she co-directed from 1995 to
2001. Previously curated exhibitions include
Liz Magor (2017), *MOON Kyungwon
& JEON Joonho* (2015), *Dorothy Iannone*
(2014), *Geoffrey Farmer* (2013), *Ragnar
Kjartansson* (2012), *Tatiana Trouvé* (2009),
Tadeusz Kantor (2008), *Rachel Harrison*
(2007), *Marc Camille Chaimowicz* (2006),
Yoko Ono (2005), and *Mark Leckey* (2003).
She teaches regularly, including at the
University of Lüneburg, Goldsmiths College
(London), the University of Bern, the
Zurich University of the Arts, and the
Jan van Eyck Academy (Maastricht). Since
1995, she has written extensively on art in
catalogues and art magazines. In 2012, she
was on the jury of the Turner Prize.

This book was published on the occasion of the exhibition *Jimmie Durham: God's Children, God's Poems* at the Migros Museum für Gegenwartskunst, August 26 – November 5, 2017.

The exhibition was curated by Heike Munder.

MIGROS MUSEUM FÜR GEGENWARTSKUNST

Director / Curator of the Exhibition:
Heike Munder
Curator:
Raphael Gygax
Head of Administration:
Catherine Reymond
Collection Curator:
Nadia Schneider Willen
Registrar / Scientific Researcher,
Collection: Anna-Lena Gugger
Registrar, Exhibitions / Scientific Researcher,
Collection: Cornelia Huth
Head of Press and Public Relations:
René Müller
Head of Education and Public Programs:
Alena Nawrotzki
Administration Assistant:
Stefanie Wolf
Art Educator:
Cynthia Gavranic
Interns:
Lea Altner, Elsa Himmer
Head of Technical Services, Exhibitions:
Monika Schori
Technical Services, Exhibitions & Events:
Markus Bösch
Technical Services, Collection:
Muriel Gutherz, Barbara Lenherr
Coordinator Media Archive:
Gabi Deutsch
Coordinator Visitor Services:
Robin Bhattacharya
Visitor Services: Yuko Edelmann, Niria
Frey, Simone Fröbel, Patricia Hanimann,
Max Heinrich, Céline Matter, Nico Meyer,
Christa Michel, Luzia Rink
Technical Services: Magdalena Battacharia,
Christian Eberhard, Cristina Golland,
Roman Gysin, Steffen Kuhn, Konstantinos
Manolakis, Emanuel Masera, Wanda Nay,
Tanja Roscic, Monika Stalder, Oli Wahmann,
Nina Weber

PUBLICATION

Published by Migros Museum für
Gegenwartskunst and JRP | Ringier

Editor:
Heike Munder
Managing Editor:
Raphael Gygax
Intern:
Lea Altner
Translation from German:
Gerrit Jackson
Translation from English:
Christian Quatmann
Copyediting and Proofreading,
German: Doris Senn
Copyediting and Proofreading,
English: Anne O'Connor
Visual Concept & Graphic Design:
Studio Marie Lusa, Marie Lusa,
Dominique Wyss
Lithography:
Georg Sidler, Schwyz
Production:
Balto, Vilnius

Thank you note by Jimmie Durham:

Looking for skulls, I enlisted the help of
many people. Everyone was generous;
Christine König, Niccolo Sprovieri, Arve
Opdahl, Pascal de Pury, Geir Tore Holm,
and Uwe Schwarzer all spent much time
looking. Kai-Morten Vollmer was, as usual,
invaluable and worked long hours with
Anita Lang to organize skulls. In the studio
day after day, William Nicholson and
Petre Petrisor lugged much heavy material;
welded, glued, tacked, nailed, and balanced a large variety of material with perfect
skill. Brad Downey and Julien Fargetton
lent a hand when needed. Heike Munder
provided everything material and mental,
her efficient, friendly staff provided expertise
and solidarity. Richard Hill, as usual, is
always intelligently helpful in many ways.

Migros Museum für Gegenwartskunst
Limmatstrasse 270
P.O. Box 1766
8031 Zurich
Switzerland
T +41 (0) 44 277 20 50
F +41 (0) 44 277 62 86
info@migrosmuseum.ch
migrosmuseum.ch

MIGROSMUSEUM
für Gegenwartskunst

An institution of the Migros Culture
Percentage. migros-kulturprozent.ch

Printed in Europe

ISBN 978-3-03764-498-0

For a list of our partner bookshops or for
any general questions, please contact
JRP|Ringier directly at info@jrp-ringier.com,
or visit our homepage jrp-ringier.com
for further information about our program.

Distributed by

JRP | Ringier
Limmatstrasse 270
CH–8005 Zurich
T +41 (0) 43 311 27 50
F +41 (0) 43 311 27 51
info@jrp-ringier.com
jrp-ringier.com

JRP | Ringier books are available interna-
tionally at selected bookstores and from
the following distribution partners:

Switzerland
AVA Verlagsauslieferung AG,
Centralweg 16,
CH–8910 Affoltern a. A.,
avainfo@ava.ch,
ava.ch

France
Les presses du réel,
35 rue Colson,
F–21000 Dijon,
info@lespressesdureel.com,
lespressesdureel.com

Germany and Austria
Vice Versa Distribution GmbH,
Potsdamer Str. 93,
D–10785 Berlin
info@viceversaartbooks.com,
orders@viceversaartbooks.com,
viceversaartbooks.com

UK and other European countries
Cornerhouse Publications, HOME,
2 Tony Wilson Place,
UK–Manchester M15 4 FN,
publications@cornerhouse.org,
cornerhousepublications.org

USA, Canada, Asia, and Australia
ARTBOOK|D.A.P.,
75 Broad Street, Suite 630,
US–New York, NY 10004
orders@dapinc.com,
artbook.com